Love, Sex, and Other
Natural Disasters

Library of Congress Cataloging in Publication Number: 2011933424

ISBN: 978-1-59474-549-2

Printed in China

Typeset in Cheltenham, Franklin Gothic, Trade Gothic, and Utopia

Designed by Katie Hatz
Production management by John J. McGurk

Quirk Books
215 Church Street
Philadelphia, PA 19106
quirkbooks.com

10 9 8 7 6 5 4 3 2 1

the ONION PRESENTS

Love, Sex

AND OTHER NATURAL DISASTERS

RELATIONSHIP REPORTING
FROM AMERICA'S FINEST NEWS SOURCE

by the Staff of
the ONION

QUIRK BOOKS
PHILADELPHIA

18-Year-Old Miraculously Finds Soulmate In Hometown

PESHTIGO, WI—In a miracle that defies statistical probability, Corey Muntner, 18, reported Monday that he found his soulmate, Tammy Gaska, right in his very own hometown of Peshtigo.

"They say God puts one special person on this planet who is your one true love," said Muntner, who has left Marinette County twice in his life, both times for marching-band competitions in nearby Menominee. "It's incredible, but I somehow found mine right here in the town where I've always lived. If that's not fate, I don't know what is."

Muntner, a 2001 graduate of Peshtigo High School, met Gaska, currently a junior at the school, in November 1999 in the student parking lot.

"I was hanging out by my car with my buddy Bryan, and this really hot chick comes walking up," Muntner said. "She asks us for a smoke, and I give her one of my Camels. So Bryan, who's a good guy but kind of a goober, says, 'What are you doing Saturday night?' She says, 'Nothing with you.' Then, for some reason, I say, 'How about me?' and she smiles and says, 'Sure.'"

Muntner and his one true love.

"That girl's name, you ask?" Muntner continued. "Tammy Gaska."

> ## "'When she told me she wanted to eat at Schussler's Supper Club, I was like, 'That's my favorite place in town!' What are the odds that out of Peshtigo's five restaurants, we'd both like the same one?'"

Relationship experts estimate that the chances of meeting someone in your lifetime that you fully connect with on a spiritual, intellectual, and physical level are one in 2.3 billion, making the geographic proximity of the soulmates nothing short of astonishing.

"How often does a person find their one true love at all, much less in the tiny rural Wisconsin town where they grew up?" Muntner said. "That's why me and Tammy are still going out even though she gave Danny [Corvo] a hand job in the Copps [Food Center] freezer a few months ago. You just don't give up on true love."

Muntner said he very nearly did not meet Gaska, making their union all the more incredible.

"When I was in 10th grade, my dad got a job offer in Manitowoc, and we almost moved," Muntner said. "If he'd taken the job, I would have never met Tammy. It's pretty scary to think about how close that was to happening. Obviously, somebody up there wanted us to be together."

Muntner said he knew almost immediately that he and Tammy were "so meant to be together."

"I could tell on the first date that Tammy was Mrs. Right," Muntner said. "When she told me she wanted to eat at Schussler's Supper Club, I was like, 'That's my favorite place in town!' What are the odds that out of Peshtigo's five restaurants, we'd both like the same one?"

While many of his friends have had to search the state, country, or at least somewhere outside a three-mile radius to find "The One," Muntner said he is doubly blessed that Gaska lives a mere four blocks away.

"My friend Rodney [Auer] has a girlfriend who lives all the way over in Oconto Falls," Muntner said. "Sometimes, he doesn't get to see her all week if something is wrong with his truck. I don't think I could stand to be away from Tammy for that long."

> ## "'That's why me and Tammy are still going out even though she gave Danny Corvo a hand job in the Copps [Food Center] freezer a few months ago. You just don't give up on true love.'"

Muntner, who prior to meeting Gaska had dated only two girls, one for five weeks and the other for two months, said he is amazed that he was able to find the perfect person so quickly—and in a town of only 3,400 people.

"Tammy is really special," Muntner said. "Most people who marry someone from their hometown just settle for whatever's around. I'm glad I didn't have to do that." Ø

Love Letter Made Longer By Increasing Margins

CRYSTAL BAY, NV—A half-page love letter written using Microsoft Word on Monday by Derek Glassburn, 19, to his girlfriend Amanda Tinker, 20, was expanded to a full page by increasing the document's margins by nearly one quarter inch on all sides.

"Even after saying that she was prettier than every girl I've ever dated, and that I loved her more than a bunch of stuff, [the letter] looked like I had put nothing into it," Glassburn said. "Besides lengthening the margins, I changed the font from Times New Roman to Helvetica, upped the font size to 12.8 points, and put it all in bold."

Glassburn reportedly handed two pages to Tinker, deciding at the last second to add a cover page with the title "Amanda Tinker: Why I Love Her, An Essay By Derek R. Glassburn."

Thousands Of High-School Sweethearts Prepare For Post-Graduation Breakup

WASHINGTON, DC—In a time-honored annual ritual, thousands of high-school seniors across the nation are cramming for final exams, trying on their graduation gowns, and preparing to break up with their longtime sweethearts.

Jeff Reidel and Amy Pocoroba, one of the nation's soon-to-break-up couples.

"Amy is an amazing girl," said Lancaster (OH) High School senior Jeff Reidel, who next week is planning to break up with Amy Pocoroba, his girlfriend of three and a half years. "I know we swore we'd be together forever, but, like me, she's got a lot of exciting opportunities ahead of her, and it just wouldn't be fair to her to keep her tied down."

Brianna Milbank, 17, a senior at Eisenhower High School in Prescott, AZ, said she plans to break up with boyfriend Chris Keegan in mid-July.

"We've already got plans for a July 4 camping trip that I'm really excited about, so I definitely want to wait until after that," Milbank said. "Chris is such an incredible guy, and these last two years have been amazing. But I just don't think I can give him what he needs right now."

> "'Amanda has the most beautiful eyes. I can't tell you how many times I've gazed into them, thinking they were the only ones I'd ever want to look into. But that was before I visied UC–Santa Cruz. The chicks there are so hot, it's not even funny.'"

As the seniors take one last look around the halls where they spent the past four years, they are also pausing to take one last look at the significant others they are about to dump.

"Amanda has the most beautiful eyes," said Trevor Hillegas of girlfriend Amanda Lum. "I can't tell you how many times I've gazed into them, thinking they were the only ones I'd ever want to look into. But that was before I visited UC–Santa Cruz. The chicks there are so hot, it's not even funny."

Hillegas said he has not closed the door on the possibility of getting back together with Lum, noting that he would still be open to the idea of the occasional hook-up with her while home during college breaks.

For most high-school seniors, graduation is the time when they cast off the remnants of childhood while accepting the challenges of adulthood. So, too, must they cast off the adolescent relationships forged by convenience, geographic proximity, and limited social opportunity.

"Jenny [Sykes] is the most beautiful girl in this school," said Brent Decker, a senior at Lake Winola (PA) High School. "But our school has only 220 students, and Penn State has, like, 40,000. There's no way she'd be the most beautiful on that campus."

Meanwhile, those slated to receive the dumpings remain confident that their relationships will endure.

"I love Zach so much," said Batavia (NY) High School senior Lisa Bracken, whose boyfriend, Zach Renfro, is joining the Navy after graduation. "He says he loves me, too, and that he'll try to get stationed near Boston where I'm going to college. I'm sure it'll all work out in the end."

Bracken added that she has not ruled out the possibility of getting pregnant with Renfro's child.

As yearbooks are passed around, signed with promises of remembrance and enduring friendship, so, too, do the seniors promise never to forget what they shared with their future ex-soulmates.

"No matter what happens, Jeff and I will always be close," said Christine Foulks, a Phoenix-area senior who plans to "break the news" to boyfriend Jeff Vanderploeg after their June 22 prom. "I just hope he doesn't expect me to give him his varsity jacket back. Or his Dave Matthews CDs."

Standing in stark contrast to the seniors are the nation's high-school juniors, who expressed horror over their elders' willingness to turn their backs on true love.

"There's no way that's ever going to happen to us," said Mindy Ostrove, 16, a junior at Tallahassee Central High School. "Matt and I are forever. Nobody else could ever understand me like he does. Nobody." ✐

A break-up note written from Omro (WI) High School senior Ronny Peltz to girlfriend Rachel Wohle.

LOVE, SEX, AND OTHER NATURAL DISASTERS

Jostens Unveils New Engagement Rings For Pregnant High Schoolers

Rise In Teen Sexual Activity Comes As Surprise To Area Teen

SALEM, OR—The Alan Guttmacher Institute released a report Friday that showed a dramatic increase in teen sexual activity, a finding that surprised policy-makers, public-health professionals, and 17-year-old Tom Ellis.

Tom Ellis, who was surprised by statistics show-ing that other teens are having sex (below).

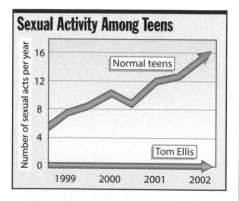

Sexual Activity Among Teens

Normal teens

Tom Ellis

"So, more teens are having sex, are they?" Ellis asked Monday. "Well, I'm not sure where those guys got all their data, but it sure wasn't from me."

Ellis, a senior this fall at Sprague High School in Salem, learned of the trend while watching television at home Saturday, as he does most weekend nights. A *20/20* story titled "The Teen Sex Epidemic" informed him that 82.6 percent of his peers aged 15 to 19 have engaged in some form of sexual contact with another person.

"Really?" Ellis asked. "Eight out of 10 teens? There's an epidemic?"

While excited by the findings on teen sexuality, Ellis has yet to observe the increase in his own life.

"I mean, it's summer, and I can't help but notice all the girls wearing sexy dresses and tank tops and stuff," he said. "But, does that mean I'm one millimeter closer to getting some tail? No, sir."

"Doesn't matter that I've grown six inches this year, that I've been working out in my basement, or that I dress in Gap clothes, like everyone else," Ellis continued. "Girls like Kelly [Mehan] and Michelle [Lehrer] still totally ignore me. At this rate, I'll be lucky to French [kiss] a girl before college."

Although teen sexual activity is on the rise, the Guttmacher report indicated that the teen pregnancy rate has dropped to a 13-year low.

"More teens are engaging in sex, but a larger percentage of them are doing so responsibly," said Dr. Jerry Kendall, a senior researcher for the Guttmacher Institute. "There's an increased access to and acceptance of proper contraceptives, mainly the condom, even among the dis-enfranchised teen population. An addi-tional factor is the marked casualization of oral sex, which is often substituted for full intercourse."

"Really?!" Ellis asked. "Blow jobs? Well, that national trend hasn't spread to Salem yet, because I'm about one blow job shy of joining that statistic. It would take a mira-cle to get a girl to go down on me."

> **"'Hey, I'm not one of those weird abstinence kids. There's nothing I would like better than to waste myself on the wrong girl. I just want to know: Where in the hell are all those millions of loose teenage girls?'"**

Ellis did confirm that he would use a condom if he were to have sex.

"You have sex, you wear a condom," said Ellis, who has practiced proper condom use alone in his bedroom. "At least that's what everybody says. I certainly wouldn't know from experience because, clearly, I'm a freak. I'm one of the pathetic 18 percent who still haven't even seen, much less touched, a naked breast. Well, rest assured: When and if I ever get the chance to have sex, I will definitely know how to put on a condom."

Although Ellis has carefully documented his intense desire for a sexual encounter in his journal, that desire hasn't translated into sexual activity. Ellis insisted that this is not by choice.

"Hey, I'm not one of those weird abstinence kids," Ellis said. "There's nothing I would like better than to waste myself on the wrong girl. I just want to know: Where in the hell are all these millions of loose teenage girls? Because they certainly don't go to my school."

According to friend Doug Binder, Ellis' chances of joining the growing ranks of the sexually experienced are slim.

"Tom?" Binder asked. "He's doomed to virginity, just like me. But, hey, that doesn't stop us from talking and thinking about sex all the freaking time. For all our yapping about what we'd do if we were ever alone with a girl, neither of us is anywhere near getting some action."

Although he admitted he was startled by the report, Ellis said he remains hopeful for the future.

"I've still got two years to get laid and join the majority," Ellis said. "I mean, I've heard guys talking about all the girls they've slept with, but I thought they were just making it up. Turns out, everyone really was having sex all that time. Well, thanks, *20/20*. Now I know what a complete loser I am." ✐

Teens who, unlike Ellis, are engaging in sexual activity.

No One Cares About Your Girlfriend Back Home

YOUR SCHOOL—No one at your new college could give even two shits about the girlfriend you left back home, a special Onion investigation confirmed Monday.

Students talking about things much more interesting than some girl you miss.

"That guy [you] acts like he's the only person in history to be separated from his high school girlfriend after leaving for college," said your roommate, who, after examining a photo prominently displayed on your dorm-room desk, described your girlfriend as being "not even that hot." "I'm sorry, but some of us are trying to actually start the next chapter of our lives here in college, so forgive me if I am not exactly on the edge of my seat about the unfolding drama of somebody's high school love."

Since relocating to your new home in the dorms earlier this month, sources report, you have gone on and on about your 17-year-old girlfriend at every possible opportunity. Worse, you have done so without apparent regard for the fact that your utterly clichéd scenario could not be less interesting to your fellow students, most of whom have spent their time hooking up with each other instead of mooning over some boring high school chick they're probably never going to see again after the next few weeks.

Students interviewed by The Onion confirmed no one cares that "this is the first time [you've] tried to make a serious go of a long-distance relationship," that "[your girlfriend] is totally worth it because she's the most special person [you've] ever known," or about any of the other things you keep going on about to anyone within earshot.

When asked to rate their interest level in your high school girlfriend, an overwhelming 93 percent of your fellow students responded "zero." Furthermore, when asked to list topics they would rather pay attention to than your girlfriend, they cited subjects ranging from dorm-safety procedures to cafeteria meal-card distribution policy to Earth Science 101.

> "When asked to rate their interest level in your high school girlfriend, an overwhelming 93 percent of your fellow students responded 'zero.'"

According to the campus-wide survey, interest was similarly nonexistent in several other areas of your life, including the fact that you were the editor of your high school yearbook, that you really miss that one cool restaurant you used to hang out at in your hometown, and that some high school buddy of yours may be coming up for a visit in a few weeks if he can get his father to lend him his car.

Your girlfriend cemented her No. 1 ranking as the least interesting subject on campus, however, when you became highly emotional about her at a party last Saturday after having what eyewitnesses said was "only, like, maybe two beers."

"[You] even told this one girl who obviously wasn't hitting on [you] that [you were] taken, and then proceeded to talk her ear off about how great [your] girlfriend is," said one of your floormates, who wished to remain anonymous for fear of being trapped in another dull conversation about your girlfriend. "What a [total pussy]."

Your girlfriend.

"Your girlfriend cemented her No. 1 ranking as the least interesting subject on campus, however, when you became highly emotional about her at a party last Saturday after having what eyewitnesses said was 'only, like, maybe two beers.'"

Furthermore, dorm insiders claimed that everyone is glad you won't be able to make it to the big get-to-know-each-other floor outing at the Cheesecake Factory this Thursday night at 8 p.m., as that is your scheduled chat time with whatever-her-stupid-name is.

Your girlfriend could not be reached for comment, as she was busy French-kissing some high school dude as of press time. Ø

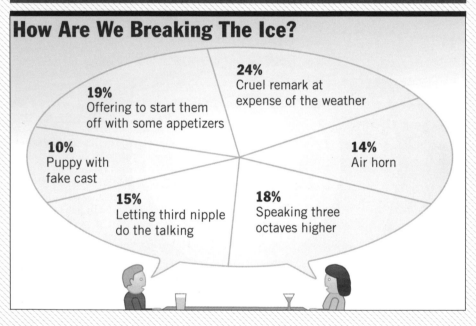

How Are We Breaking The Ice?

24%
Cruel remark at
expense of the weather

19%
Offering to start them
off with some appetizers

10%
Puppy with
fake cast

14%
Air horn

15%
Letting third nipple
do the talking

18%
Speaking three
octaves higher

I've Left My Haltingly Awkward Voice Message; Now The Ball's In Her Court

As a single guy who's gotten out there a fair amount, I've learned how to play the game. The way I see it, if someone's interested, great. If not, no skin off my nose. Take last night: I got the number of this hot young thing at a bar and decided to give her a call. And now that I've left my painfully uncomfortable six-minute-long voice message on her cell, I'm not going to waste my time obsessing over my next move. The ball's in her court

By Vince Gazno

If she wants to make the next move and return my panicked and barely coherent phone message, that's fine by me. If not, she can take a hike.

See, I've laid the groundwork, and if I do say so myself, it was pretty fucking painful: I stared blankly at my phone for a few hours; I dialed the number and said hello but in a voice so low that I had to clear my throat and repeat it several times; I spent a full minute awkwardly trying to explain that I was the guy drinking vodka tonics, but then, realizing that other people she was talking to were drinking gin and tonics, which look pretty similar, I said that maybe she'd remember me as the one wearing a bomber jacket and singing along to most of the songs that came on the jukebox; after that, I sealed the deal by stuttering my own name a half dozen times before spitting out "Vince."

Or did I say Victor?

Look, I could be a total loser and stay up all night waiting for her to get back to me, and I almost certainly will do that. But, why bother? If she calls, she calls. I put my sweaty, desperate cards on the table, and now it's on her. And unless I'm mistaken—which I usually am—as soon as she hears the sound of my trembling voice she'll be digging through her purse for the Arby's receipt that I frantically scribbled my name and number on.

What can I say? I guess my voice just has that effect on some women.

And when she does call, I am not going to freak out like it's the first time a woman's ever called me or something. In fact, I may just let it ring and keep her on ice for a while, assuming I don't panic first and start screaming into the receiver the second I hear the phone ring.

> ## "After that, I sealed the deal by stuttering my own name a half dozen times before spitting out 'Vince.' Or did I say Victor?"

Because I'm the kind of player who likes to come on too strong. Just a nice, pitiful, borderline disturbing phone message, and I'm on with my life. It's not like I invited her and her sister to come have tacos with my parents and me tomorrow night or anything. At least, I'm pretty sure I didn't. To be honest, the last few minutes of the message were kind of a blur.

All I'm saying is, if she wants to get in touch with me, she knows how to reach

> **"I just hope that she doesn't communicate by fax machine. If she does, well, then, tough cookies, because I don't have one. That's just how I roll."**

me. After all, when I left the voicemail, I helpfully supplied her with my cell phone number, my home number, my work number, both my e-mail addresses, and my old pager number. I even repeated the info twice so she could find a pen and paper and write it all down. I just hope that she doesn't communicate by fax machine. If she does, well, then, tough cookies, because I don't have one.

That's just how I roll.

Hey, if she doesn't want to come over to my tiny, filthy apartment for a brief round of underwhelming, surprisingly messy sex, then that's her loss. Really, it's cool. I got a whole line of girls ready to politely exchange numbers with me as I stare at my feet, too petrified to make eye contact. It's not like I'm hard up for females or anything, someone whose breasts I can clumsily fumble over until, in disgust and disappointment, she makes up an excuse to leave.

Yes, sir, I'll just be here hanging out, playing it cool, and checking my voicemail messages every 45 seconds or so. No big deal. No big deal whatsoever.

Unless you think something went wrong with her voicemail and she couldn't retrieve my message. Could that have happened? Huh. You know what? Maybe I should call her back real quick. Just in case. Yeah. Just in case. *Ø*

Gay Couple Has Banal Sex

MINNEAPOLIS—Jerome Ostrowski and Barry Lipner engaged in the practice of banal sex Monday, sources reported. "After we got home from Don Giovanni's, the restaurant we go to pretty much every Monday night, Barry started giving me one of his predictable mood-setting backrubs," Ostrowski said. "After five minutes of that, he mounted me and put in a hundred or so quick thrusts. All in all, not one of our more memorable encounters." Lipner said that Ostrowski's reciprocal act of fellatio was "serviceable."

Dating Tips

The dating world can be a bewildering place. Here are some tips to help you navigate the perilous waters of love:

- Ladies: Your date's salary divided by your own equals the base you should let him get to on the first date.

- If you are overweight and socially awkward, consider "online dating." You can go on a dragonslaying adventure instead of to a movie, play games on Pogo.com instead of dancing, and masturbate instead of having real sex.

- Do not bathe for several days prior to a date to get your pheromones good and strong.

- Never date a married person, unless he or she is just about to leave his or her spouse and simply waiting for the right moment.

- When planning a romantic candlelit dinner, the right music can create the perfect mood. Put on *The Best Of Spike Jones* to create a freewheeling, anything-goes atmosphere.

- Maintain a casual, "Let's just have fun" attitude until the other person starts seeing someone else. Then let the tears and accusations fly.

- Remember: There's only one way to console a widow.

- To make a lasting impression on a first date, declare yourself his or her eternal soulmate and propose marriage.

- Why don't you ask that Julie girl out? She's a lovely girl. You're practically 35, for God's sake. Fine, rip your mother's heart out.

- If you are a princess being courted by a low-born but beloved suitor, be sure to elude the watchful eye of the lord high chamberlain.

- Instead of going out tonight, punch yourself in the nuts three times and the heart twice. This will save you approximately $75.

Heaven Must Be Missing An Angel Or Something To That Effect

By Aaron Kaplan

Excuse me, beautiful, mind if I stand next to you and do some talking? I don't mean to intrude, but I couldn't help but notice that you were sitting all alone and enjoying yourself. There's just one problem: If you're here right now, then that means heaven must be missing an angel or something to that effect. Though I doubt anyone's noticed since there are so many angels up there anyway.

I'm trying to say that you're hot. You look pretty tired, though. Maybe it's because you've been running through my mind for a while. I think about hot women a lot, so for the purposes of this argument let's just say you were one of the ones that I'd previously been thinking about, even though we just met. Are you considering having sex with me yet? Because if not, I could ask you if it hurt when you hit the ground after falling from heaven. I know I already said the thing about you being an angel, but maybe you didn't catch it the first time. Or if you did, maybe it will seem like I'm building off that. I'm trying to tell you that you're pretty like an angel I want to sleep with, is the point.

What else is there? Oh, are you from Tennessee? Because I think you're a seven. I might have gotten that wrong, but you get the gist of it. I'm using the name of a state to express how much I'd like to see you naked, but I don't really care where you're from.

Can we just go now? All right, well then why don't you tell me your sign. I don't really believe in astrology, but maybe you do and will go home with me because I come across as open-minded for mentioning it. I think I'm a Virgo. Pisces? One of those. I'm sure we'd be good together, because you're very attractive, as I've said before, which I think is really the most important thing anyway. Speaking of which, do you have a license? Because you're driving me somewhere that's complimentary to you.

> ## "Are you from Tennessee? Because I think you're a seven. I might have gotten that wrong, but you get the gist of it. I'm using the name of a state to express how much I'd like to see you naked, but I don't really care where you're from."

Your eyes are blue like the sky or water, whichever you prefer. And your lips are really red like—I don't know—that girl's lips over there. Also, I'd look great cumming on your shirt. Or your shirt's becoming, I mean. I want to be cumming on your shirt or in your general vicinity is what I'm getting at. I didn't quite say it right, but the sentiment is there.

So do you have a boyfriend or what? Because I don't have all night to waste on talking to you if you're dating someone.

> ## "Do you come here often? If so, would you like to go back with me to my apartment and have sex with me? What if I told you I would rearrange the alphabet for some reason?"

Do you have a mirror in your pocket so I can see myself in your pants? How about a quarter, so I can call my mother and tell her I found the girl of my dreams? I'm not actually going to call her, because she's been dead for two years and it's actually up to 35 cents now anyway and I'd probably just use my cell phone, but I'll take the quarter from you if it will get you in the sack.

We should go back to my place and do some math. We'll add a bed, subtract our clothes, and do other math stuff related to fucking.

Look, it's obvious where this is leading. I'm saying all the right things and you haven't walked away yet, so let's just cut to the chase: Do you come here often? If so, would you like to go back with me to my apartment and have sex with me? What if I told you I would rearrange the alphabet for some reason? I'm thinking of asking you what you'd like for breakfast tomorrow, in the hopes that you might sleep with me because I implied that it's inevitable.

Can you see where I'm going here?

I guess I should say I think I've seen you someplace before. And I don't mean earlier, when I was staring at you. I'm pretty sure we've met in a past life or in my dreams or something, so you should feel comfortable lowering your standards around me. Also, your shoes are nice, so I'm sensitive and observant. If you really need me to, I could buy you a drink to show you I have some money and then we could do it in the bathroom.

Wait, don't go. Just one more thing. I lost my phone number. Can I have yours so I can call you later about having sex? Ø

Man Breaks Out Dating Boxers

SUFFOLK, VA—Having secured a date for the first time in seven months, area resident Andrew Agee removed his dating boxers from the bottom of his dresser. "No tighty-whities for me tonight," said Agee, taking off a pair of dingy Fruit Of The Loom briefs and slipping on the blue Calvin Klein boxers with a small, understated white "CK" logo near the bottom of the right leg. "A girl might actually see me in my underwear." Agee added that if the date goes well and future encounters with the woman seem likely, he will purchase a three-pack of boxers.

20,000 Tons Of Pubic Hair Trimmed In Preparation For Valentine's Day

WASHINGTON—Flushed with anticipation and ready to emerge from another long, cold winter, millions of Americans participated this week in the annual tradition of trimming their pubic regions in time for Valentine's Day.

Americans all across the country once again prepared for Valentine's Day by carefully thinning their pubis.

A ritual as old as time itself, this year's pubis-shearing is expected to be among the largest in decades, with more than 20,000 tons of curly clippings predicted to fall by Feb. 14.

"My boyfriend and I are going to see As You Like It and then enjoy a nice candle-lit three-course dinner," said Brooklyn resident Lydia Simonson, who along with many other hopeful lovers will soon excuse herself from her daily duties, retreat to a nearby bathroom, and carefully tend to the area around her genitalia. "It's going to be so romantic!"

Indeed, tiny scissors and electric razors have already begun to fly off drugstore shelves, while all across the country legs are dangling precariously over open bathtub drains. According to statistics from the National Depilatory Council, the week before Valentine's Day is by far the busiest time of the year for shaving, trimming, sculpting, playful pattern-making, waxing, and even manscaping.

"David and I are going to take a long walk around the park and then maybe on the way home we'll stop and grab some ice cream," said Julie Stibbons, a Dallas-area design consultant who recently made use of grooming shears, a pair of tweezers, and two magnifying mirrors to contribute her 0.4 ounces to the nation's total raw tonnage. "I wonder if David will send me flowers at work like last year."

Added Stibbons, whose smooth vaginal region will show no signs of stubble for days to come, "He's just so wonderful."

> **"In 1947, the first year records were kept, Americans only mowed about 1.25 tons off their 'crotch lawns,' while in the mid-1970s private trimmings were so rare that documentation was actually abandoned until 1981."**

While this year promises to be prolific, experts said the country has gone through many personal grooming phases over the years. In 1947, the first year records were kept, Americans mowed only about 1.25 tons off their "crotch lawns," while in the mid-1970s private trimmings were so rare that documentation was actually abandoned until 1981.

But with the booming economy of the 1990s, the U.S. saw a significant resurgence in pre–Valentine's Day shearing and plucking.

"There's a huge spike every year in the first half of February," said Brooks Watson, who is head of sales at Schick, makers of the TrimStyle razor for women. "The rest of the year, Americans generate about 50,000 tons of total trimmings, but in the week before this special holiday we see a massive jump. It's a veritable clear-cutting down there."

"Bzzzzzzzz," he added. "Timber!"

According to Schick's marketing research, during the Valentine's season, U.S. pubic hair removal rates briefly approach those of Brazil, traditionally the smoothest country on the planet. While Americans seem willing to chop it all off for their annual celebration of romance, personal trimming still varies by season and plummets to levels almost as low as Greece's during the week of Thanksgiving.

"If I trim the shrubs, the tree looks bigger," said Jeremy Wertz of Boise, ID, standing in front of his hall mirror with a pair of scissors taken from his employer's supply closet. "See? Worth the itching, if you ask me."

While many consider the practice a time-honored tradition, not all Americans share Wertz's enthusiasm.

"I'm not going to let corporate America dictate the date or time at which I choose to groom my genitals," said Denver resident Marcus Shannon, adding that Valentine's Day was "invented by the razor industry" to sell grooming devices. "If you really love somebody, you should shave your pubes year-round."

"While Americans seem willing to chop it all off for their annual celebration of romance, personal trimming still varies by season and plummets to levels almost as low as Greece's during the week of Thanksgiving."

Meanwhile, National Depilatory Council director Donna Spaulding said the sudden nationwide surge in follicular concern is understandable, but she urged caution.

"We all want to look good and feel desirable, but it's important to keep things in perspective," Spaulding said. "In the end, you want people to love your pubic region for what's inside, not just for how it looks." ⊘

Area Man Thinks Girlfriend's Sister Might Be A Little Cuter

CANTON, OH—Local resident Matt Holm expressed fear Monday that Sheri Glass, sister of girlfriend Amanda Glass, might be a bit cuter. "Sheri's got a slightly smaller nose, and her breasts are better," a distressed Holm told a male friend after seeing the two sisters side by side for the first time. "And, even though I haven't seen it, I strongly suspect that her stomach is more toned." Holm has not yet decided whether to break up with Amanda.

Area Man Creeped Out By Request To 'Make Love'

WINSTON-SALEM, NC—A half-naked Patrick Fuller was thoroughly creeped out Saturday, when fellow Wake Forest University senior Alicia Echols suggested that the two "make love."

Patrick Fuller

"There we were, messing around on the couch in her apartment's living room," Fuller said. "Things were heating up, so I asked if we should go back to her bedroom in case her roommate came home. That's when she stood up and said, 'Make love to me, Patrick.'"

"It was really weird," continued Fuller, who met Echols three weeks ago and had gone on two dates with her prior to Saturday. "I mean, Alicia's definitely not the type of girl who'd say, 'Let's fuck.' But still: 'Make love to me'? That's very different than saying, 'Let's have sex.'"

"What did she mean by 'love'?" Fuller asked. "We're not even dating. I mean, we've gone out a few times, so I guess we're sort of technically casually dating, in a way, but it's not like she's my girlfriend."

Fuller said he was further creeped out when, upon entering the bedroom, Echols told him she was "ready to take you inside."

"I was thinking, this is getting kinda heavy," Fuller said. "We were just gonna have some sex, and for some reason, she's talking about it like our two souls are about to intertwine or something."

Fuller said he and Echols had kissed on their previous two dates, but nothing else. He also noted that he thought they "weren't even hitting it off all that well," which made Echols' behavior Saturday all the more surprising.

> "'I was thinking, this is getting kinda heavy. We were just gonna have some sex, and for some reason, she's talking about it like our two souls are about to intertwine or something.'"

"The moment I got to Alicia's apartment, things seemed strange," Fuller said. "She had all these scented candles lit, and there was a bottle of wine to go with the spaghetti she'd made. The radio was even turned to the classical-music station. It was really inappropriately romantic. We're not, like, deep, impassioned lovers or anything like that."

"I was totally up for having some fun," Fuller said. "But then, all of a sudden, she starts talking about how 'incredibly special this night is' and how she's 'ready to open myself up to you.' I totally wasn't prepared. Did she expect me to say stuff like, 'Darling, you look radiant tonight'? Was I supposed to bring flowers? You don't do that when you're just having a little fling."

Fuller said he doesn't know what the future holds for him and Echols. For now, he simply plans to wait and see if "everything is cool."

"I don't know how things will go next time I see her. There were definitely some weird vibes Saturday night, that's for sure," Fuller said. "The sex was still pretty good, though." *

> "'Did she expect me to say stuff like, 'Darling, you look radiant tonight'? Was I supposed to bring flowers? You don't do that when you're just having a little fling.'"

Boyfriend Vows To Try Harder

BREMERTON, WA—Area resident Len Wallace made a solemn vow Monday to girlfriend Mindy Ellis that he would try much, much harder. "I've just been going through so much crazy stuff these days, baby," Wallace said. "From here on out, I'm gonna be the best boyfriend in the world." Wallace added that they're going to spend so much time together, he swears to God.

New Roommate Hopes Five-Hour Fuckfest Didn't Keep You Up

OSHKOSH, WI—Roommate Brian Penderman, 26, announced Monday morning that he hopes the loud bumping, grinding, and moaning of the five-hour-long fuckfest he had with his girlfriend did not in any way prevent you from sleeping last night.

"I'm exhausted—are you exhausted?" Penderman asked while he extended his arms in a stretching motion and yawned loudly. "Honestly, though, I sincerely apologize if all that fucking that was going on in my bedroom kept you up until the early hours of the morning."

Penderman, who moved into the apartment last September based on your buddy Dave's insistence that he was an all-right guy, was never pressed for details, but openly volunteered information regarding the fuckfest's length, the nakedness of his girlfriend, and the number of times they "did it." According to sources in the apartment, Penderman's most recent fuckfest was also his first fuckfest since moving in.

"Just so you know, we didn't plan this or anything," said Penderman, referring to the self-described fuckfest that took place between approximately 9 p.m. and 2 a.m. "Out of respect for you, we were just going to have a quickie. In fact, I was done and ready to go to sleep after 20 minutes, but she kept begging for more."

Added Penderman: "You know how chicks can be."

Confessing that the fuckfest had taken

Penderman gets some much-needed calories after repeatedly satisfying his girlfriend, all night long.

a considerable toll on his body, Penderman voiced numerous complaints ranging from aching arms to chafed knees to a sore penis. Penderman went on to explain that the reason his penis was so sore was because it had repeatedly entered and exited a female vagina the night before.

> ## "Penderman, who moved into the apartment last September based on your buddy Dave's insistence that he was an all-right guy, was never pressed for details, but openly volunteered information regarding the fuckfest's length, the nakedness of his girlfriend, and the number of times they 'did it.'"

While his girlfriend reportedly hurried out of the apartment at 7 a.m. in order to return to her hometown of Shawano and was therefore unavailable for comment, Penderman apologized on her behalf for all the loud, crazy sex noises you must have been hearing. Penderman admitted, however, that he was not prepared to discount the likelihood of another fuckfest occurring very soon.

"I can't say it won't happen again, because she's talking about taking the bus down here in August," Penderman said. "You might want to go away that weekend. But if you are around, I'll slip a note under your door saying 'Having fuckfest' and you'll know."

"Not that you wouldn't know anyway," he added, despite your repeated insistence that you in fact slept very well. "As you might have noticed, she's a bit of a moaner."

Though Penderman established that he has not seen you bring home anyone in months, he stated that he would not be opposed to you having a fuckfest.

"This is your home, you should be able to bang all night long anytime you want—like I did," Penderman said. "I'd be happy to ask my girlfriend if she knows anybody who might be interested in you."

Throughout the day and then again that afternoon when you returned home from running errands, Penderman continued to express regret that "this place reeks of sex," which he blamed equally on the considerable amount of intercourse he was having over and over again yesterday and the apartment's thin walls. Penderman added that he would be glad to buy a scented candle or air freshener at the store this evening, when he goes to replace the large number of condoms he used the previous night.

"Fuckfests are not all fun and games, my friend," Penderman added. "It's a lot of hard work just to keep going on and on and on. I mean, you heard us, right?"

Before your departure from the apartment for the night, Penderman offered to have an open discussion about the fuckfest "when you're ready," in order to answer any questions you might have about the fuckfest and to assure you that he will try to conduct future fuckfests in a way that will not cause you to feel uncomfortable or jealous to be living with a guy who gets it so regular. ∅

Man Adds A Few Personalized Tracks To Standard New-Girlfriend Mix CD

SPRINGFIELD, MO—Wanting to add something special for new love Danielle Welter, Andy Mansfield, 24, burned three personalized tracks Monday onto his standard new-girlfriend mix CD. "Danielle loves that No Doubt song 'Running,' so I threw that on there just for her," Mansfield said. "And she doesn't really like rap, which [previous girlfriend] Erica [Hollings] loved, so I took off [Salt-N-Pepa's] 'Whatta Man' and replaced it with two Aretha Franklin songs, because Danielle loves the oldies." Mansfield said he expects Welter to love the mix "even more than Erica did, maybe even as much as Christine."

Bar Skanks Announce Plan To Kiss

COLUMBUS, OH—In an announcement that received wide attention throughout Wolverine's Tavern Tuesday, bar skanks Stephanie Fletcher and Jessica Keneally stated that they would share a passionate kiss at an unspecified time that evening.

"Steph and I are totally hot for each other," Keneally said over the loud music to several unspecified bar patrons. "We're going to make out. We don't care who's watching."

According to eyewitnesses who looked up the second they walked in the door, the 22-year-old skanks arrived at the bar at approximately 10 p.m, dressed in their usual skank attire of low-cut tank tops paired with either low-rider jeans or a short skirt, and exposed, brightly colored thongs.

After downing their third cosmopolitans, the two skanks stood up and began grinding to the R. Kelly song "I'm a Flirt," which caused a nearby conversation about the Cleveland Indians to come to a sudden halt.

"Quit staring," Keneally said to the approximately 25 male patrons in the immediate vicinity, all of whom were by that time involuntarily ogling the skank-ass pair. "Oh my God, you guys are such pervs."

Fletcher would neither confirm nor deny that the kiss would involve tongue, saying that bargoers "would just have to wait."

"Who knows what will go down," Fletcher said as she reached into Keneally's tight top and tweaked her left breast with her thumb and middle finger in front of seven rapt onlookers. "Possibly us."

In previous months, Keneally and Fletcher have, either separately or together, shown off their lower-back tattoos, held a loud conversation about who had the larger breasts, and displayed their

The skanks pose for one of the hundreds of pictures taken over the course of the night.

oral sex techniques on bottles of Bud Light. Neither is a lesbian.

"'You mean the one that flashed her tits last week is gonna make out with the girl who was telling everyone she wasn't wearing any underwear? Whatever.'"

"Those chicks are all over each other—awesome!" said 24-year-old Matt Lalley, one of dozens of slightly intoxicated males who, despite their highly evolved brains, were unable to stop looking at the suggestive twosome. "This is going to be the best night of my life."

As the evening wore on, the skanks' hair grew lank and stringy, increasingly clinging to their sweaty faces despite frequent coquettish head tosses. The heat and close quarters of the small bar also caused the sparkly body makeup worn by Fletcher to collect in the crevices of her collarbone and between her breasts. According to Wolverine's bartender Helene Dorman, the skanks also left thick hot pink lipstick prints on their drink glasses.

However, none of these factors resulted in any decrease in the amount of attention paid to the skanks.

"I just can't look away," said Frank Sturm, watching as Keneally leaned over the pool table to display her plunging neckline for the ninth time. "And the thing is, the one in the skirt isn't even all that hot."

"I'd really like to think I'm above this," Sturm's friend, Greg Kleist, added. "But what can I say? I'm not. They're totally going to kiss."

Not everyone was as enthusiastic about the pair's announcement. A 28-year-old female bar patron rolled her eyes at the girls' predictable antics, and was immediately dismissed by Fletcher and Keneally as "jealous." The bartender reported that she'd seen similar scenes play out on countless other evenings.

"You mean the one that flashed her tits last week is gonna make out with the girl who was telling everyone she wasn't wearing any underwear?" Dorman asked while setting out newly washed glasses. "Whatever."

As of press time, the pair had still not kissed, as they were rumored to be waiting for someone to buy them another drink before astonishing onlookers with their shocking intra-gender lip-lock. Ø

Girlfriend Loves Spending 'Alone Time' With You

SAGINAW, MI—According to your girlfriend, your request for some "alone time" this afternoon sounds fantastic, and she'd love nothing more than to do that with you. "We could go to the farmers market, or even just read in the park together," your girlfriend said. "Or we could go on a long walk by ourselves. This is great we haven't had any alone time in months." Sources close to your girlfriend said she has already contacted two other couples she knows, to see if they're free to do a small alone-time thing around 8 p.m.

Dream About You Not Sexual, Coworker Reports

BURLINGTON, VT—In an impromptu conversation held in the elevator of your office building Monday, coworker Andrew Pagano announced that he had a dream about you the previous night. In the moments following the announcement, Pagano added that he "just thought you'd find that funny" before assuring you that the dream wasn't what you're thinking.

Pagano describes his "completely platonic" dream.

"I just thought it was weird, just because you and I have been working so many hours together on this Hendricks account, and now you're popping up in my dreams," said Pagano, chuckling nervously and taking a single step back. "Ha, no, totally G-rated."

He then issued a number of additional statements in rapid succession, confirming that you had all your clothes on, the dream was really short, and it was actually one of those dreams where no one has faces. Upon reaching the door to your office, witnesses said, he playfully slugged you on the shoulder and walked back to his cubicle.

According to company records, Pagano graduated from Pennsylvania State University in 1991 with a degree in marketing, and since May 2005 has worked in your office as a senior account manager. In the past three years, he has had an estimated 18 separate dreams featuring you; however, this is the first time the 39-year-old has acknowledged one publicly.

> **"In the past three years, he has had an estimated 18 separate dreams featuring you; however, this is the first time the 39-year-old has acknowledged one publicly."**

"Really, I have dreams about people from work all the time," Pagano said less than an hour later, when he returned to your desk to reiterate the complete lack of erotic undertones in his dream. "It wasn't like that. My friend Paul was there, too."

"Besides, it's not like I can control what I dream or anything," he continued. "Not that you needed controlling in it. It's—do you dream a lot, too?"

Despite your assurances that everything was fine and that you were not mad, just working, Pagano persisted in his attempts to convince you of the dream's innocence by describing what you both were doing in the dream—working together at a Baskin-Robbins—and questioning how logical it would be to tell you about a dream if it were a sex dream.

"Don't worry, if I ever had a dream where you and I were…you know, like that, I'd keep it to myself," Pagano said. "Not that it has happened. Because it hasn't. Because if it had, I'd tell you now, obviously. Because, you know, I brought it up, and, yeah."

He then attempted to change the subject to last week's staff meeting with CFO Mark Gentry, but, after several moments, abandoned the new conversational direction to clarify that it wasn't because you're not a very attractive woman.

"I really got to cut out the spicy foods before bedtime, is what it is," Pagano said. "I've been having the craziest dreams ever since my divorce."

> "'Don't worry, if I ever had a dream where you and I were . . . you know, like that, I'd keep it to myself. Not that it has happened. Because it hasn't. Because if it had, I'd tell you now, obviously.'"

You have not spoken to Pagano since he coincidentally ran into you in the parking garage after work, but sources report he is expected to "make it up to you" tomorrow at lunch, when he drives across town and purchases you a cookie from your favorite bakery. ⌀

Last Great Party Of Life To Result In First Child

LAKE CHARLES, LA—Unbeknownst to him, 27-year-old Ron DuPree attended the last great party of his life Saturday, as a 3 a.m. coupling with girlfriend Tamara Harris will result in a child nine months from now. "That was the best party ever," DuPree said to friends on Monday, oblivious to the seed of life now growing in his soon-to-he-wife's womb. "I was so wasted! God, Tamara and I have to start getting out on the weekends again." In addition to enjoying his last great party, DuPree will also soon bid farewell to liquor, cigarettes, and most of his current friendships.

Casual Sex Surprisingly Formal

DAYTONA BEACH, FL—After several hours of drunken Spring Break revelry Monday, Ron Viselic, 19, and Becky Pell, 18, returned to Pell's motel room for surprisingly formal casual sex. "We were laughing and doing body shots at the bar, but when we got back to my room, things turned all businesslike," Pell said. "He kept asking me if it was okay to take off each piece of clothing, then he wouldn't do anything but missionary." Following the methodical, strangely businesslike intercourse, Viselic and Pell spent five minutes "spooning" before Viselic dressed and left.

Ex-Girlfriend Don't Want To Speak To You No More, New European Boyfriend Reports

LANCASTER, PA—According to the latest information provided by the unnamed, impossibly debonair-sounding European man who is now answering all of her calls, your ex-girlfriend, Rebecca Norsten, "don't want to speak to you no more."

The olive-skinned baron.

The new policy of non-communication, not elaborated upon by Norsten herself, was announced during a phone call to her apartment early Monday morning in the suave, confident tones of an Italian or possibly Portuguese individual of indeterminate height and muscle tone. Phone records indicate the statement was made at 9:35 a.m.—approximately one hour and 25 minutes too early for the speaker to have been a platonic visitor who did not spend all last night giving the love of your life everything you never could.

"Rebecca is no coming to the phone, my friend," reported the exotic-sounding stranger, who rolled his R's in a manner that strongly suggested he can outperform you sexually. "I am condolence for you, but what is to be done? There are many fishes, yes?"

> "'Rebecca is no coming to the phone, my friend,' reported the exotic-sounding stranger, who rolled his R's in a manner that strongly suggested he can outperform you sexually."

The probable Mediterranean sex god concluded the statement by saying "ciao," after which it can be assumed he returned to his previous task of hand-feeding your ex-girlfriend slices of juicy mango while she reclined naked in a hammock, finally free from the burden of dating you.

Although no answers have been provided to your flabbergasted stutterings following the announcement, 17 hours of careful overanalysis did uncover several new, emasculating details from within the one-and-a-half-minute conversation. It is now believed that the olive-skinned baron and multiple-vineyard owner who relayed the message is currently living with and possibly married to the woman you once tried to impress by wearing a belt.

You have also been able to deduce, without the aid of visual confirmation, that Norsten's new European boyfriend was dressed in flowing white linen pants and rustic kidskin loafers, and is, at this very moment, slowly consuming a perfectly ripened orange.

"It must be really hard for her to talk so soon after we broke up," you have repeatedly told yourself to drown out images of the black-haired Adonis laying your ex-girlfriend upon a bed of imported silk cushions, removing a string of freshly killed quails from around his broad shoulders, and riding your beloved Becky like she was the last boat to America. "I'm sure this guy, whoever he is, is just a one-time thing. She'll probably explain everything next time we talk."

The announcement that communication would cease immediately came as a shock to everyone whom Norsten had previously promised to "love forever and ever." The 24-year-old Notre Dame graduate was

> **"It is now believed that the olive-skinned baron and multiple-vineyard owner who relayed the message is currently living with and possibly married to the woman you once tried to impress by wearing a belt."**

your girlfriend from November 2007 to May 2008, and in that time made no mention of plans to visit Europe and had no European friends or coworkers. Upon closer recollection, however, it has been noted that Norsten once watched the entirety of Once Upon A Time In Mexico with you, more than twice commenting on actor Antonio Banderas' "sexy accent."

As of press time, it is unclear how you could have been so foolish. ✐

How Did We Meet Our Significant Other?

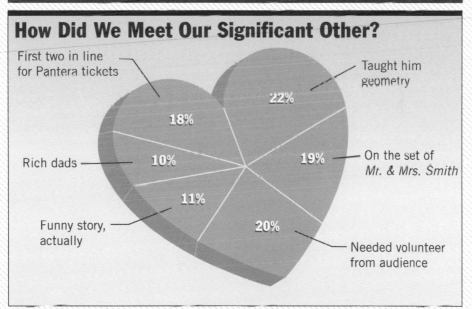

First two in line
for Pantera tickets

Taught him
geometry

22%

18%

Rich dads

10%

19%

On the set of
Mr. & Mrs. Smith

11%

Funny story,
actually

20%

Needed volunteer
from audience

Date Disasterously Bypasses Physical Intimacy, Goes Straight To Emotional Intimacy

CHAPEL HILL, NC—An initially promising date between University of North Carolina seniors Mike Rafelson and Jill Zehme veered disastrously off course Monday night, when the two skipped directly to intense emotional bonding, tragically bypassing the physical intimacy that usually precedes it.

"It's not what you think—unfortunately," Rafelson told his roommates Tuesday morning after they watched him send Zehme off with a long, tight goodbye hug and an affectionate kiss on the forehead. "The date was going great—I could feel us getting closer and closer all night. I was totally psyched when she came home with me. But somehow I screwed up, and we ended up sharing our most personal thoughts and feelings without even making out first."

Rafelson said he and Zehme met two weeks ago at Raleigh's Schoolkids Records, where they spent 20 minutes wandering past each other while pretending to look at vintage LPs, self-consciously brushing bangs

Zehme and Rafelson share a close moment.

back from their foreheads, and stealing glances at each other over the display racks.

Rafelson said he "finally made a move" and asked Zehme about the album she was holding, *Talking Heads: 77*. In the 20-minute discussion that followed, Zehme not only told Rafelson how important the album had been to her during a troubling time in her adolescence, but that she worked at a local coffeehouse.

> ## "As he and Zehme continued to talk, they spoke more passionately, their faces got closer together, and they began to stare intently into each other's eyes."

"She went out of her way to describe the location of the Buzz Café and the hours she usually works," Rafelson said. "I was, like, 'Yeah! This is it, man—she totally likes me and I'm gonna get some action.' Unfortunately, I was only half right—and it was the wrong half."

After he "happened to swing by" Buzz Café, Rafelson asked Zehme if she would like to see his friend's band, Chat!, thus launching the pair's ill-fated journey to non-physical intimacy.

"When I picked her up, she looked really hot," Rafelson said. "After the show, we went to get some pizza, and our feet were touching under the table the whole time we ate. We talked for a long time about the trouble she was having finishing up her major, and I could totally relate. Everything seemed to be progressing so nicely. Well, I didn't know it at the time, but the feet thing was the closest physical contact we were going to share."

At 12:30 a.m., as the couple walked to Rafelson's place, their conversation grew more personal. Rafelson talked about his last girlfriend, and Zehme discussed her financial problems. At his door, Rafelson said his roommates would not be home until later, and to his delight, Zehme agreed to come inside. Rafelson opened a bottle of wine, and the two sat talking and drinking in the living room for an hour before relocating to the bedroom.

The bedroom, Zehme later told friends, is where she and Rafelson "started to open up about just everything."

"From the moment I laid eyes on Mike, he seemed like the kind of guy I could really get close to," Zehme said. "He had such a sincere way about him—a face I could totally trust."

> ## "Two and a half hours later, the couple was firmly in the area that couples therapist Gus French described as 'that awful horse latitude of male-female relations, the Sargasso Sea of non-sexual pair-bonding known to unhappy males the world over as 'the friend zone.'"

Rafelson said it seemed that, given the circumstances, some form of sexual bonding was assured. As he and Zehme continued to talk, they spoke more passionately, their faces got closer together, and they began to stare intently into each other's eyes.

"The intimacy in the room had worked its way to a fever pitch," Rafelson said. "But before I realized what was happening, disaster struck."

Instead of stroking her date's thigh or taking off her shirt, Zehme began to tell Rafelson things she'd "never told anyone outside of [her] closest confidants."

"I told Mike all my innermost feelings about my parents' traumatic divorce, my brother's drug problem, and my best friend's attempted suicide," Zehme said. "He was so sweet—he took my hand and told me to let it all out. And I did. I just let it all go. I was totally uninhibited that night. I've never been like that with anyone before."

Two and a half hours later, the couple was firmly in the area that couples therapist Gus French described as "that awful horse latitude of male-female relations, the Sargasso Sea of non-sexual pair-bonding known to unhappy males the world over as 'the friend zone.'"

"My heart really goes out to this poor kid," French said. "We've all been there, thinking, 'Gee, this is really special that you're opening up to me about your childhood, but I've got to admit I'd rather be going down on you right now.' Unfortunately, once the emotional barrier has been crossed, there's no going back. By allowing the conversation to swerve into serious-talking territory before physical contact was established, Rafelson virtually guaranteed that he would not get into Zehme's pants."

Rafelson corroborated French's prediction.

"Jill said our date was one of the most special nights of her life," Rafelson said. "We talked long into the night until we fell asleep side by side—fully dressed. In the morning, before leaving, she gave me a huge, sincere, and utterly asexual hug—exactly the kind of hug someone would give her brother." ∅

New Girlfriend Bears Disturbing Resemblance To Old Girlfriend

ATLANTA—Friends of David Buntrock told reporters Monday that his new girlfriend Katie Wickstrom looks unsettlingly similar to his former girlfriend Tonya Gill. "When I first saw them together I thought, 'Wow, did David and Tonya work things out?'" friend Angie Lisota said, explaining that both Wickstrom and Gill are petite, with cropped brown hair, big eyes, and a penchant for dressing like ballet dancers. "Even her voice sounds a little nasally, like Tonya's." According to Buntrock, Wickstrom "actually looks more like Audrey Hepburn."

Nike Introduces New Intercourse Shoe

BEAVERTON, OR—In yet another first for the world's premier athletic footwear manufacturer, Nike announced Tuesday the nationwide launch of the Air Fornicator, a lightweight copulating shoe designed to maximize sexual performance.

The newly released Air Fornicators promise better traction during coitus.

"Nike is proud to continue its commitment to new and innovative products with the first ever sneaker developed exclusively for sex," president and CEO Mark Parker said. "Stylishly sculpted and contoured for enhanced comfort, the featherlight Air Fornicator provides superior energy return to reduce fatigue and boost the libido."

"With this shoe you will last longer, experience more pleasure, and fuck smarter," Parker added.

According to a Nike press release, the Air Fornicator's cutting-edge support system creates maximum foot stability, which in turn improves coital alignment, increases clitoral stimulation, and deepens penetration. The revolutionary midsole component reportedly works to adapt to the user's pelvic motions and cushions the overall shock of repetitive grinding.

Retailing for $175, the Air Fornicator will be available in high-tops and low-tops and in a variety of passion-inducing color schemes.

Senior Nike footwear designer Barry Hudson said the shoe's outer sole was constructed from a durable carbonized rubber to improve grip, enhance traction, and prevent slipping on a variety of surfaces, including carpeting, concrete, wallpaper, hardwood, and silk. In addition, Hudson claimed that the rounded CliMax-brand air heel facilitates more efficient thrusting and lustful pounding.

> "The shoe's outer sole was constructed from a durbable carbonized rubber to improve grip, enhance traction, and prevent slipping on a variety of surfaces, including carpeting, concrete, wallpaper, hardwood, and silk."

"We made dozens of adjustments to the tread pattern to ensure balance, as well as proper support for arched backs," Hudson said. "And the soles were designed to minimize sliding around in bodily fluids. You can make love standing up in a puddle of massage oil and you won't fall down."

Nike's research department performed thousands of trials on the Air Fornicator over a 16-month period, including a number of stamina tests and other off-site experiments intended to gauge the intercourse shoe's robustness. Engineers, who observed couples in a variety of sexual positions, found several cases in which the Air Fornicator suddenly flew loose during intense coitus, a problem they remedied by tightening the lacing pattern and adding a Velcro strap for security.

A nationwide marketing campaign for the copulation sneaker will debut this Friday with a 60-second television ad scheduled to air on all major networks. The ad, shot in black-and-white and accompanied by the Led Zepellin song "Whole Lotta Love," features a montage of several slow-motion scenes. These include a shot of a sweat-covered man pleasuring his wife, who reaches climax seconds later, shattering their bed's headboard; a high-angled pan of a woman rolling her wheelchair up a steep hill while making love to her partner;

and finally, a close-up of an Olympic runner, who bends over to lace up his Air Fornicators, before the camera pulls back to reveal his teammate approaching from behind with a strap-on dildo.

Sales for the new shoe are expected to be strong.

"My wife enjoys it when I make love to her, but I usually wind up feeling tired and sore," focus group volunteer Michael Nelson said. "Since getting the Air Fornicators, though, I've been giving it to her all the time. It hardly even feels like fucking anymore."

While Nike marketers found that consumers responded favorably to the product's claim of helping them "get into the erogenous zone," a small percentage were still not convinced.

"I'm not going to spend $175 on an intercourse shoe when I only have sex like once a month at most," Dallas native Erica Graham said. "They would probably just sit in the closet and gather dust." ❧

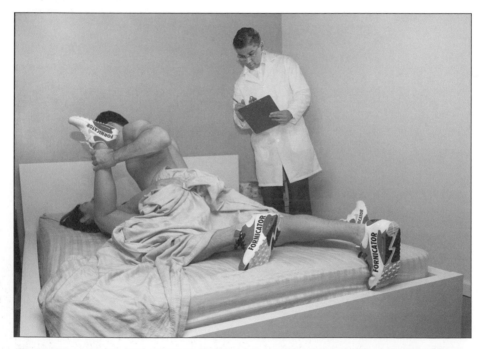

Nike design engineers subjected the Air Fornicators to a battery of erotic tests on multiple surfaces.

4-Year-Old's Idea Of Barbie, Ken Marriage Involves Lots Of Head Collisions

Supportive Gay Friend To Counsel American People On Ways Of Romance

WASHINGTON, DC—Reeling from countless relationships gone awry, blind dates from hell, and one-night stands that were about one night too long, the American people received help Monday in the form of tart-tongued but shrewdly perceptive gay friend Garrett Blaine.

Sassy, supportive gay man Garrett Blaine vows to be there for the American people.

At a White House Rose Garden ceremony, President Bush named Blaine, 30, U.S. Romance Counselor-General. Charged with dispensing no-nonsense relationship advice to more than 250 million Americans, as well as providing citizens with a shoulder to cry on, Blaine will summon every ounce of his energetic, outgoing personality and gift for outrageous one-liners.

"All Americans—not just stylish urbanites—should have access to a sassy, supportive gay sidekick with whom they can share their romantic trials and tribulations," Bush said. "It is as basic a right as a good education or complete medical coverage."

Blaine, who when not attending to wounded veterans of the dating wars works at the Racy Stamen Floral Boutique & Oxygen Bar in Los Angeles, attempted to explain his knack for helping heterosexuals with their love woes.

"A lot of people ask me, how does a gay man know so much about solving straight people's romantic problems?" Blaine said. "Honey, if I knew the answer to that, I'd be God. And I know I'm not God, because I'm not black or female! Well, not black and only about a quarter female."

Continued Blaine: "I can always tell when something's wrong with the U.S. populace when they come into my shop. Their posture's drooping, or they avert their eyes, or they tell me they love my new turquoise polka-dotted shoes. Oh, boy! That's when I know something's wrong. So I roll up my sleeves, brew up a big pot of java, haul the cheesecake out of the fridge, and say, 'Okay, American people, this is Garrett you're talking to here. What's eating you? And don't say 'a Brazilian cabana boy,' because I won't believe you."

> **"'Honey, if I knew the answer to that, I'd be God. And I know I'm not God, because I'm not black or female! Well, not black and only about a quarter female.'"**

In the years prior to his appointment, Blaine tirelessly supported nearly 8,000

Americans as they braved the roller-coaster ride that is modern romance.

> ## "'He told me to take a chance on that nerdy-but-nice tech-support guy at work, because, as Garrett put it, 'He may wear a *Star Trek* necktie, but he's better than those Klingons you've been dating!'"

"If it weren't for Garrett, I'd probably be with yet another guy who's more committed to his health-club membership than to me," said Alyssa Ennis, an insurance-claims adjuster from Saginaw, MI. "Instead, he told me to take a chance on

that nerdy-but-nice tech-support guy at work, because, as Garrett put it, 'He may wear a *Star Trek* necktie, but he's better than those Klingons you've been dating!'"

Continued Ennis: "Neil and I have been together for more than a year, and we just got engaged! Thanks, Garrett!"

Another American who has benefited from Blaine's help is Santa Fe, NM, bookstore employee Andrea Adkins. In 1996, Adkins was 100 pounds overweight and involved with a man who constantly derided her appearance.

"I was very unhappy with this guy," Adkins said, "but I felt that, looking the way I did, beggars can't be choosers."

Outraged by Adkins' predicament, Blaine closed his shop and moved in with her. "I took one look at Andrea," Blaine said, "and I immediately thought, now there's a gal who needs a flamboyant, frank-talking sidekick."

Over the course of the next year, Blaine coached, coaxed, and cajoled Adkins down to a svelte 110 pounds. He also encouraged her to pursue the open position of children's-section manager at her bookstore and helped her gain enough self respect to dump her no-good boyfriend once and for all.

"Garrett saved my life," Adkins said. "There has been a 180-degree turnaround

Blaine offers support and encouragement to La Crosse, WI, brewery worker Bob Sharpe, whose wife recently cheated on him.

in the way I look at things. Instead of being the beggar, now I'm making them beg. As Garrett says, 'You go, girl!'"

Blaine's clientele is not entirely female. Brad Cochrane of Shreveport, LA, contacted Garrett in November after a second attempt to reconcile with his girlfriend failed.

> ## "'At first, I was kind of uneasy about Garrett's homosexuality. But after I found out he probably never actually does it with a man, he became safe and non-threatening.'"

"When I picked up Garrett at the airport, the first thing he did was put his hands on his hips, cluck his tongue, and say, 'Brad, old buddy, do we ever have our work cut out for us,'" Cochrane said. "I had no idea what he was talking about. But then he gave me the news."

Blaine, Cochrane recalled, bluntly informed him that his number-one roadblock to reconciling with his girlfriend was his slovenly wardrobe.

"We went straight to the mall, where I tried on clothes as ZZ Top's 'Sharp Dressed Man' blasted over the P.A.," Cochrane said. "Garrett chose enough Armani suits and Hugo Boss casual wear to outfit an army. I told him I didn't have enough money for all

that stuff, but Garrett just said, 'Baby, you just need to hop on board a certain train called the American Express.'"

After receiving a crash course in etiquette from Blaine, Cochrane unveiled his new look to his girlfriend at a fancy French restaurant. Sure enough, she agreed to give him another chance.

"I'd still be sitting home alone in my pizza-sauce-stained sweatpants if not for Garrett," Cochrane said. "He's a real straight shooter."

Informed of Cochrane's use of the adjective "straight" in describing him, Blaine emitted a mock shriek.

Though Blaine is renowned for his skills as a pal and confidante, little is known about his own love life.

"Garrett has been out of the closet for years, but I can't remember him ever having a steady boyfriend or even a date," Adkins said. "In fact, I've never even seen him kiss a man. Isn't that strange? It's almost like he's asexual."

"At first, I was kind of uneasy about Garrett's homosexuality," Cochrane said. "But after I found out he probably never actually does it with a man, he became safe and non-threatening."

Blaine will have his work cut out for him Thursday, his first official day in his new position: Karyn Robles of Grand Junction, CO, has not yet told her boyfriend that she hates his new moustache. Joe Barents of Huntington, NY, is still waiting in vain for a phone call from a lingerie model with whom he had a blind date two weeks ago. And Meredith Crouch of Durham, NC, was recently asked to dinner by her boss, with whom there has long been a simmering mutual attraction, but she feels it might jeopardize her career. Should she or shouldn't she?

"Hold the fort, buckaroos," Blaine said. "It's Garrett to the rescue!" ✐

Cosmopolitan Releases 40-Year Compendium: 812,683 Ways To Please Your Man

Study: Casual Sex Only Rewarding For First Few Decades

ARLINGTON, VA—An alarming new study published in the International Journal of Sexual Health reveals that casual sex, the practice of engaging in frequent, spontaneous sexual encounters with new and exciting partners, may only provide unimaginable pleasure and heart-pounding exhilaration for, at most, 25 to 30 years.

This couple may be having fun now, but there could be cause for regret a quarter-lifetime later, researchers say.

"People who choose to participate in random, no-strings-attached lovemaking sessions with sexually adventurous strangers should be advised that this type of behavior is only incredibly liberating for the first quarter-century or so," said Dr. Loren Sullivan of Yale University, who coauthored the study on the long-term side effects of living out one's wildest fantasies on a semi-weekly basis. "Though sometimes it can be longer."

The study observed 100 sexually active volunteers who were not tied down by dull, passionless relationships and were therefore able to have sex with whomever they wanted, whenever they wanted. A control group of individuals who were married or had otherwise allowed their erogenous zones to fall into complete and utter numbness was also monitored for comparison.

Researchers found that those who regularly achieved mind-blowing orgasms without the expectation of commitment often experienced mild feelings of loneliness and a passing regret after as little as three decades of pure physical bliss free of emotional complication.

> **"'People who choose to participate in random, no-strings-attached lovemaking sessions with sexually adventurous strangers should be advised that this type of behavior is only incredibly liberating for the first quarter-century or so.'"**

"There's a troubling number of adults who spend their prime sexual years in complete coital abandon, then have nothing to show for it but dozens upon dozens of highly detailed erotic memories," Sullivan said. "They must be so empty inside, one would think."

Other common, albeit latent, secondary effects noted in the study include mild disappointment and mid-afternoon crankiness, as well as a lingering need for additional casual sex. Researchers could not conclusively establish a link between anonymous, passionate trysts in nightclub bathrooms and these results, however, as a large portion of the polling group was found to be asymptomatic.

One participant, California native Greg Pertzborn, told researchers he sometimes wonders if the 30 years he spent beneath a different gorgeous woman every night were worth the periodic flickers of gloominess he began experiencing at the age of 59.

"When I think back on the countless times I've had raw, almost bestial sex, indoors or outdoors, with one, sometimes two Asian women whose parents I'll never have to meet, I occasionally get a little down," Pertzborn said. "God, what if I wasted my life having guilt-free, uninhibited, sensually explosive sex with anyone I wanted?"

Sullivan and his team plan to continue the study, saying they expect to find that the unattached, sexually satisfied persons between the ages of 20 and 30 whom they have been monitoring will feel compelled to settle down with a single partner and begin discussing joint checking accounts "any day now."

"Tragically, it's quite possible that many of these singles may never realize how miserable a lifetime of phenomenal, kinky sex can make them," said Sullivan, adding that recent evidence suggests such a healthy, rational realization could be further hindered by the experience of spontaneous oral sex behind the bushes at poolside cocktail parties.

Although the study has not yet caused any perceptible reduction in the popularity of having casual sex, proponents of the report, like husband and father-of-four Howard Kehoe, say it provides proof that promiscuity is not "the endless carnal thrill-ride" it is often made out to be.

"I am so thankful that I never acted on my natural impulses and engaged in a sweaty, toe-curling, life-affirming romp with that knockout I saw in the park last week," Kehoe said. "I may die having only caressed the naked, goose pimpled flesh of two women on the entire planet, including my wife, but at least I know I'll never have to endure a burst of fleeting regret long after I've retired."

"That's one sensation I never want to experience," Kehoe added. &

Valentine's Day Coming A Little Early In Relationship

MONROE, MI—Area resident Todd Munde, who has been dating Lisa Watroo for the past three weeks, lamented Monday that Valentine's Day is coming a little early in the couple's relationship. "It's kind of weird to be doing the whole romantic flowers-and-candy Valentine's Day thing with somebody you just started seeing," said Munde, 30, "Ideally, we would have started dating last October. That way, Valentine's Day would have fallen somewhere around the four-month mark. Oh, well."

Horrified Man Looks On Powerlessly As He Ruins Date

DAYTON, OH—What was intended as a routine first date went horribly awry Tuesday night as local man Kevin Parker, 29, could do little more than stand by and watch himself ruin his chances with 28-year-old Vanessa Carmine.

Parker says there was nothing he could do to stop himself from mentioning his former bed-wetting problem.

Parker told reporters that the date at a local restaurant began pleasantly and without incident. The two enjoyed small talk right up until the salads arrived, at which point disaster struck, and an unsuspecting Parker discovered he was powerless to stop himself from droning on like an idiot about his recent car troubles.

"It was awful," Parker said of the date, his first in more than eight months. "One minute we were getting to know each other, and the next I was sitting there in shock, hearing myself ramble for what seemed like hours about how I'd been meaning for months to get my oil changed, but I kept putting it off, and then when I finally took it in the guy at the auto shop charged me more than the estimate, and how you have to be careful because mechanics are always trying to rip you off, and isn't it a

shame that people can't just be honest."

"God, the look on Vanessa's face," added Parker, shaking his head. "I'll never forget it."

As soon as he realized what was happening, Parker sprung into action, attempting to rescue the evening with amusing childhood anecdotes, but only exacerbating the situation by discussing his parents' divorce and his former bed-wetting problem. After

A Disaster Unfolds

6:55	Parker arrives at the restaurant five minutes before Carmine, completely oblivious to the catastrophe that is about to unfold
7:12	Orders are taken; Parker has a glass of red wine to take the edge off
7:18	Waiter presents the salad; fresh ground pepper joke goes nowhere
7:19	Parker feels the first trickle of perspiration go down his back
7:27	Parker inadvertently upends his glass of wine, breaking the stem of the glass and cutting his thumb on a jagged edge
7:29	Realizing that the bleeding isn't going to stop, Parker excuses self to go to the restroom
7:33 - 7:35	Longest point of awkward silence
7:41	Parker remarks that passing woman resembles ex-girlfriend, thus initiating lengthy explanation of how over the relationship he is
7:44	Carmine excuses self to go to restroom. Assuming he's been deserted, Parker drains wine and orders another, only to have it arrive after Carmine returns
7:52	Parker makes mouth-guitar noises
7:59	Realizing he's made a terrible mistake, Parker breaks personal record for consuming a dessert and coffee

knocking over a glass of wine as he asked Carmine where she was from, Parker realized saving the night from total disaster might be beyond his power.

Summoning his strength for one last heroic effort, Parker said he began talking about his dog, found himself unable to discuss anything beyond how the pet had been his only comfort during a breakup last year, and then proceeded to spend

> ## "'I remember looking around the room thinking, 'For God's sake, somebody do something!' Then I just sort of went numb for a few minutes there as I watched myself talk about my laundry schedule.'"

five minutes explaining how he was "totally over" his ex-girlfriend now.

"There was this loud, disturbing noise, and I realized it was my own voice," Parker said. "I remember looking around the room thinking, 'For God's sake, somebody *do* something!' Then I just sort of went numb for a few minutes there as I watched myself talk about my laundry schedule."

"At one point, Vanessa got up to use the restroom, and I thought that maybe she wasn't coming back," Parker continued. "That it would finally all be over."

When the unthinkable happened and Carmine returned, Parker gave up all hope and began sweating through his dress shirt while talking about his love of death metal.

"The entire date was a massacre," Parker said. "The waiter couldn't even make eye contact with me. He knew what was happening. He should have thought to bring the check instead of the dessert menu. Or at the very least, he should have kept me from prolonging the agony by ordering the apple dumpling and offering to split it."

"I wish I could forget everything I witnessed here tonight," Parker added. "But it's burned in my memory forever."

At press time, Parker was walking Carmine to her car, insisting it was no problem despite Carmine's protestations that it was not necessary. Ø

Woman Masturbates To Concept Of Commitment

PORTAGE, MI—Soaking in her bathtub Tuesday, area resident Linda Marston, 32, pleasured herself over the thought of a long-term committed relationship "Mmmm... oh, yeah, baby... I want to settle down with you forever," moaned the never-married Marston, as she gently massaged her clitoris with two fingers. "Oh, God, yes... two kids, maybe three... and a house in the country. Big swingset in the backyard." Several hours later, Marston masturbated again to the idea of loving someone unconditionally through good times and bad.

Americans Marrying Later

Census Bureau figures for 2003 show that Americans are getting married later, with the average age for a first marriage having risen to 26. What do *you* think?

Dale Steele
Systems Analyst

"Oh, great. First my grandmother starts pestering me about not being married, then my parents, and now the national media."

Lois Halverson
Real Estate Clerk

"Thank God there's a greater trend I can look to when I ponder my lonely, loveless existence in the midnight hour."

Curtis Fuller
Salesperson

"I don't have to worry about marriage at this point in my life. Paying child support for three kids is stressful enough as it is."

Ruby Turpin
Auditor

"It's because of the sluggish economy. It's harder to get a dowry together these days."

Marvin Watts
Robotics Technician

"Christ. Get ready for some of the bitterest-looking bridesmaids in history."

Glen Powers
Home Health Aid

"My folks got married at 17. They were also cousins. Let me know when you have your tape recorder ready."

New Six Flags Ride Based On Relationship With Deborah

VALENCIA, CA—Promoting the coaster as "the most heartbreaking ride on earth," the Six Flags Magic Mountain theme park unveiled its newest attraction this week: a 395-foot-tall steel roller coaster designed to simulate a grueling three year relationship with Deborah.

Developed by world-renowned and recently single engineer Phillip Werner, the Life Force Crusher-X is said to feature six disorienting vertical loops, 150-feet of highly unstable barrel rolls, a portion in the middle where the ride just suddenly stops for no reason and refuses to start again until riders apologize, and an unexpected 310-foot drop at the very end.

"This heart racing, gut wrenching 90 mph free fall into unhealthy codependence and trust issues will have even the most extreme thrill-seekers begging for it to be over," reads a Six Flags press release announcing the new coaster, which promises to require more attention and patience than any one man should reasonably be expected to have. "Can you survive the Agonizing Vortex of Unflagging Acrimony?"

According to park officials, the coaster begins with an impulsive burst of acceleration that, when riders reflect upon the experience years later, will prove to be the only enjoyable portion of the ride. A series of unexpected and painful twists rapidly follow, leaving riders confused, strangely resentful, and wondering if they made a huge mistake getting on the ride in the first place. For the next 25 minutes, the coaster creeps endlessly forward at an agonizing pace, until it actually starts moving backward.

The first drop fills riders with exhilaration tinged with abject fear of what's to come.

When the Life Force Crusher-X mercifully comes to an end, park visitors often find themselves speechless, emotionally exhausted, and completely broke.

"What the fuck just happened?" roller coaster enthusiast Derek Schumer said. "At first things were great, but next thing I knew, I was throwing my hands in the air and screaming, 'Why are we even doing this? I don't understand why we're doing this! It doesn't make either of us the least bit happy. Just end it, already, just end it!'"

Added Schumer, "I think I'm going to be sick."

Despite opening only last week, Life Force Crusher-X is already one of Magic Mountain's main attractions. The park has even been forced to extend its hours to accommodate ticket holders who said they would never come back, only to find themselves pounding on the gates at 2 a.m., desperate for just one more go-round.

"I can't decide if I hate the ride or hate myself for going on it," read one comment on a website that reviews roller coasters. "At one point I glanced over at the people on other coasters, and they all looked so much happier."

"I don't know," the comment continued. "Maybe the Life Force Crusher-X is just the type of coaster I deserve."

Park-goer Andrew Murray had a similar experience on the Six Flags ride.

"Pretty early on, I realized that I just needed to get off," Murray said. "But by that point we had just passed through the Tunnel of Pregnancy Scares, and there was no way I could up and leave then. God, to think of all the other rides I could have tried if I weren't trapped on that suffocating machine."

Although some have expressed safety concerns with the coaster's structure—more than 7,000 feet of steel tubular track hastily built on a foundation of lust and shared contempt—both Six Flags and the designer himself have assured riders that

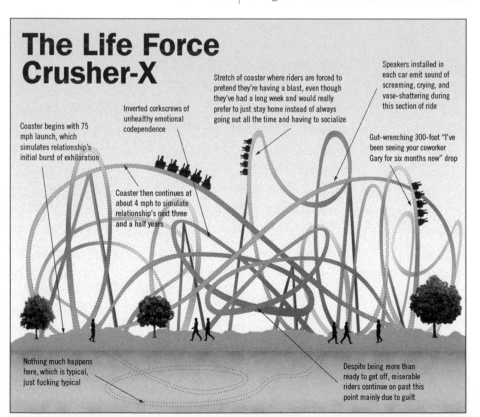

The Life Force Crusher-X

Coaster begins with 75 mph launch, which simulates relationship's initial burst of exhilaration

Inverted corkscrews of unhealthy emotional codependence

Coaster then continues at about 4 mph to simulate relationship's next three and a half years

Stretch of coaster where riders are forced to pretend they're having a blast, even though they've had a long week and would really prefer to just stay home instead of always going out all the time and having to socialize

Speakers installed in each car emit sound of screaming, crying, and vase-shattering during this section of ride

Gut-wrenching 300-foot "I've been seeing your coworker Gary for six months now" drop

Nothing much happens here, which is typical, just fucking typical

Despite being more than ready to get off, miserable riders continue on past this point mainly due to guilt

> **"'I can't decide if I hate the ride or hate myself for going on it. At one point I glanced over at the people on other coasters, and they all looked so much happier.'"**

the Life Force Crusher-X is nowhere near as dangerous as actually dating Deborah.

"Every inch of my coaster has been biodynamically analyzed by computers to be 100 percent safe, which is far more protection than I ever got from that heart-swallowing banshee of a woman," designer Werner said at the unveiling of his semi-autobiographical ride. "In fact, I myself ride the Crusher every morning. Just to remember."

Six Flags officials said they've already begun construction on their next coaster, one they are calling "even more terrifying than being in a relationship with Deborah."

It's scheduled to open in 2012 and will be based on not being in a relationship with Deborah. *Ø*

Former Couple To Remain Friends Until One Finds New Sex Partner

MCMINNVILLE, OR—Bryce Tornquist and Stephanie Herrick, whose three-year relationship ended in August, are remaining close friends until one of them finds a new sex partner. "We still have a lot in common, and it's really nice to have someone around who knows you so well," the 26-year-old Tornquist said Tuesday. "So, until one of us is having sex with somebody else, it really works out for both of us." Tornquist added that he really, really hopes to be the one to find a new sex partner first.

SWM May Have Lied About Liking Sunsets, Long Walks

NEW LONDON, CT—According to reports, Steve Zollner, 36, a New London–area non-smoking SWM, may have lied about his taste for long walks and sunsets.

A June 1996 file photo of non-smoking SWM Steve Zollner sharing good times and outdoor fun with an unidentified woman.

Zollner's long-walks- and sunset-liking claim, which has appeared frequently in the personals section of *The New London Examiner* since late December, is believed by local police to be part of an elaborate scheme by the at-large Zollner to lure unsuspecting attractive, fit SWFs between the ages of 30 to 40.

"Lurking somewhere in this city is a scam artist who lures innocent women to his voice-mail box with false claims of enjoying sunsets, long walks, and various other activities of a romantic nature," New London police chief Eugene Woodall said. "We are urging all women in the area to exercise extreme caution when approaching unfamiliar men for friendship and possibly more."

> "'A well-built outdoors-type who loves spending cuddly evenings in front of the fireplace and going out to movies? It just didn't seem possible for one man to have so many wildly divergent interests.'"

In addition to sunsets and long walks, Zollner, who sometimes goes by the aliases "Classy Companion" and "Your Mr. Right?" claimed in the 58-word ad to have a fondness for candlelit dinners, close companionship, and new adventures. Zollner's numerous victims said these claims are also false.

"In the ad, Steve sounded like a real teddy bear, so I called him up," said Rhonda

Leland, a petite 36-year-old veterinarian's assistant who is intelligent and independent, but also a dreamer. "Then, after a few weeks of dating him, it became clear that Steve wasn't interested in anything but drinking beer and watching *COPS*. Once, I even suggested that we go for a walk and he said, 'Walk? What do you want to walk for?' It was obvious that I had been the victim of a scam."

Shoe-store manager Janet Dreisbach, a once bitten, twice shy, recently divorced professional with above-average looks, had a similar experience with Zollner. "When I saw #2567's ad, it seemed too good to be true," said Dreisbach, who has been looking for a discriminating soulmate for good times and great conversation since February 1996. "After all, it sounded like we had a lot in common, like the part in the ad that said he 'enjoys having fun.' Well, as I quickly found out, it was too good to be true."

Thus far, police said, Zollner's scam has claimed eight victims. In addition to Leland and Dreisbach, six other women responded to Zollner's personals ad during its five-week run, including three who actually went on dates with Zollner and one who left several messages for him on *The New London Examiner*'s automated Love Line.

"Something about this particular personals ad just didn't add up," said Det. Daniel Stenson, who launched the investigation of Zollner after spotting his ad in a special Jan. 3 "Catch The Love Bug" pullout section of *The Examiner*. "A well-built outdoors-type who loves spending cuddly evenings in front of the fireplace and going out to movies? It just didn't seem possible for one man to have so many wildly divergent interests."

Also being sought by police is Erik Larsen, a friend of Zollner's who is widely suspected to be the individual who suggested that Zollner try placing a personals ad. According to police, Larsen also may have assisted Zollner in writing the ad, in effect making him an accomplice to the crime.

"Serving as an accomplice to fraud is a serious crime with serious consequences," Stenson said. "If Mr. Larsen is caught, he will have some very grave questions to answer."

Though no formal charges have yet been filed against Zollner, police have collected substantial evidence against him. For example, contrary to Zollner's claim of being "a major music lover," a police search of his home found that he owns only six CDs, one of which is a Little River Band disc still in its plastic shrink-wrap. Further, Zollner's assertion that he loves "drinking wine by the fireplace" was cast into doubt when investigators found no trace of either wine or a fireplace in his three-room apartment.

> ## "Contrary to Zollner's claim of being 'a major music lover,' a police search of his home found that he owns only six CDs, one of which is a Little River Band disc still in its plastic shrink-wrap."

"It is clear that by concocting these deliberately misleading fabrications, Zollner intended to represent himself in a positive light to overly trusting members of the opposite sex," Stenson said. "And for what purpose? To ensnare them in the cruel web of banality and boredom that is his existence as an aging single."

Anyone with information about Zollner is urged to call the New London Police Department at 1-900-555-9365, box #2952. Callers must be 18 or older, and all calls are strictly confidential. Touchtone phones only. No fatties. 𝄐

Goth, Metalhead Overcome Subcultural Differences To Find Love

DANVILLE, IL—People fall in love every day, but self-proclaimed "Goth for life" Danielle Richardson, 24, and avid metal-music fan Rick Halloway, 26, faced bigger obstacles than most couples. In spite of having come from vastly different subcultural groups, the unlikely couple celebrated their three-month anniversary Monday.

Rick Halloway and Danielle Richardson, who overcame odds to find love.

"It hasn't been easy dating someone so totally different," said Halloway, wearing faded black jeans and a Mastodon T-shirt. "There have been times, like when Dani asked who Phil Anselmo was, that I almost wanted to say 'forget this bullshit.' But then I reminded myself that nothing good is ever easy. That's why I chose the path of metal—living fast and rocking hard. I never in my craziest dreams thought that path would lead me to Dani, but I'm so glad it did."

Added Halloway: "Fuckin' A, she totally rocks."

Richardson said that, although she has lived her whole life in the same small, largely middle-class Midwestern town as Halloway, the two couldn't be more different. While Halloway spends his free time fixing his car or plugging the jukebox at T.J.'s Tap, Richardson spends her free time shopping at thrift stores and reading poetry at The Black Cat, a red-velvet-curtained bar nearly 10 blocks away from T.J.'s.

"No one is more surprised by our union than I," Richardson said. "When we met, there was a strong attraction, but so much more is required for lasting love. I never believed one such as Rick could touch my shadowed heart, but touch it he has."

> **"'Danielle was wearing this black lacy thing. I like women who wear black, but usually it's leather with studs. But something about her made me wait for her after my movie got out.'"**

Halloway admitted that the relationship got off to a shaky start.

"Me and some of my friends were hanging out in front of the Midas when Dani walked by with a big, black umbrella," Halloway said. "Well, it wasn't raining, so my friends started making fun of her. But when she looked over, our eyes locked. I was like, 'Whoa.'"

A few days later, Halloway ran into Richardson at the Danville Cineplex.

"I asked her what she was going to see—I think it was that gay-ass *Blade: Trinity* movie," Halloway said. "Danielle was wearing this weird black lacy thing. I like women who wear black, but usually it's leather with studs. But something about her made me wait for her after my movie got out. I'm so glad I did."

> "'I thought Danielle was just trying to get a reaction from us by going out with some loser. I could see how our outrage might be delicious to her, but now, she actually seems serious about Rick. This lunacy makes my mind swim with sadness.'"

Richardson said she began dating Halloway with serious reservations.

"Our first date was positively chilling—Rick's soul seemed to be crying out to me," Richardson said. "Still, it brought me much pain to realize that we would have no future together—we were so very different."

"But at the end of the night, when I reached out to take Rick's hand, I noticed that his fingernails were painted black," Richardson added. "I told him how sexy it was, and he told me he got the idea from a Danzig video. That was the first time I realized we had something deep and eternal in common."

Although he had similar doubts, Halloway said he "decided to say 'fuck it' and go for it."

"On our next date, Danielle took me to this place where a house had burned to the ground—the whole place was all scorched and shit," Halloway said. "It looked like a Sepultura video. It was such a kickass spot that we started making out like animals."

Continued Halloway: "For a girl who writes poetry, Danielle is a totally crazed hell-demon in the sack. She tears the shit out of my back. She's a righteous chick, even if she doesn't like me calling her that."

Although the couple overcame subcultural differences, their friends have not been so open-minded.

"I thought Danielle was just trying to get a reaction from us by going out with some loser," said Valerie Brasher, a longtime Goth. "I could see how our outrage might be delicious to her, but now, she actually seems serious about Rick. This lunacy makes my mind swim with sadness."

"Danielle will always be very dear to me, but I can't support that relationship," Brasher added. "Once, I suggested that Rick wax his goatee into a tapered, devilish point and he told me to keep my pale-ass freak hands to myself. I mean, talk about your typical close-minded metalhead vulgarian behavior."

Halloway's friends have similarly disparaged the union.

"I told Rick that there's a reason why, when we were all in high school, our friends would hang out under the bleachers and the Goths would hang out in the atrium," Mike Kryzinski said. "It was because our kinds don't get along. What's gonna happen at their wedding when Danielle starts playing Sisters Of Mercy or some shit like that? What kind of music are their kids gonna listen to? Hasn't he ever stopped and thought about the future?" Ø

Woman Only Dates On National Television Now

HOLLYWOOD—After stints on *Temptation Island*, *The Bachelor*, and *For Love Or Money*, 23-year-old bartender/model Angela Langdon announced Monday that she refuses to date anyone who's not courting her in a front of a national TV audience. "Unless there's the promise of a million-dollar payday, a romantic evening in the tropics, or a humiliating rejection in front of all of America, I'm not interested," Langdon told potential suitors. "Come with cameras, or don't come at all." Langdon also expressed a preference for network shows over those in syndication.

Soulmate Dropped For New, Better Soulmate

BLOOMINGTON, IN—The deep and abiding love shared by soulmates Andrew Colton and Brenda Smolensk ended Monday, when Colton broke up with Smolensk to go out with new soulmate Mandy Damrush.

Soulmates Andrew Colton and Mandy Damrush. Inset: Brenda Smolensk, Colton's former soulmate.

"Mandy and I are so perfect together, I almost can't believe it," a beaming Colton said Monday. "It's like we're the same person. Even though we just met, I feel like we're soulmates, like I've known her my whole life."

From June 17, 1996, until 2:15 p.m. Monday, Colton and former soulmate Smolensk were inseparable, describing themselves as "unwhole without each other." In a poem he gave to Smolensk in June to commemorate the third anniversary of their meeting, Colton described their relationship as "like one mind in two bodies, ever understanding and ever clear."

According to Colton, Smolensk was the love of his life at the time.

"Brenda and I were a perfect match,"

Colton said. "We would go on long walks and talk for hours about literally any subject. I would start a sentence, fumble for a word, and Brenda would finish for me. Or she could just look at me and say out loud what I was thinking."

Added Colton: "Fortunately, Mandy doesn't interrupt me or do any of that annoying stuff Brenda did."

Colton also fondly recalled his last Christmas with Smolensk. "One of my gifts to her was a Thighmaster, and she got all excited and asked, 'How did you know I wanted to work on my thighs?'" Colton said "How did I know? Well, I would often see her standing in front of her full-length mirror and, just from the way she looked at

> **"'I want to be clear that I'm not trying to bad-mouth Brenda at all. I have nothing but good things to say about her. What we had was truly once-in-a-lifetime. But what I have now is even more once-in-a-lifetime.'"**

herself, I could tell she was unhappy about all the dimples in her thighs. That's just the sort of deep understanding we had for each other."

Colton then slipped his arm around Damrush and said, "Mandy has got incredible thighs."

But despite the fact that the pair's relationship seemed made in heaven, Colton and Smolensk gradually grew apart.

> ## "'Mandy is so incredibly wonderful. I mean, I thought Brenda was the only woman in the world for Andrew, but now it's clear that it's Mandy.'"

"As great as Brenda was, we somehow fell into a rut. Toward the end, we didn't do anything together. We didn't even talk very much," said Colton, recalling his last days with Smolensk. "On the other hand, Mandy and I already get along so well, it's like we have a telepathic bond—neither of us even has to say a word. Mandy truly is the only person on the planet I can see myself with. What are the odds we would meet?"

Colton's friends have already accepted his newer, even more ideal companion into their circle.

"Mandy is so incredibly wonderful," said David Rudd, Colton's best friend and roommate. "I mean, I thought Brenda was the only woman in the world for Andrew, but now it's clear that it's Mandy."

"I know it sounds like a cliche, but Andrew and Brenda were so right for each other, it seemed like it was, like, cosmic or something," longtime friend Marc Elliot said. "Believe me, the last thing anyone expected was that Andrew would actually find a soulmate who was even better."

"Good for him," Elliot added.

Despite having moved on, Colton stressed the special place his ex-soulmate will always have in his heart: "I want to be clear that I'm not trying to bad-mouth Brenda at all. I have nothing but good things to say about her. What we had was truly once-in-a-lifetime. But what I have now is even more once-in-a-lifetime."

Colton said he will always be thankful for meeting Smolensk, as he learned much from her.

"When fate led me to Brenda, I was a wounded person, afraid I would never again be able to trust a woman. After all, my heart had been broken by three previous soulmates," Colton said. "But Brenda taught me that I could find true love again. And you know what? That's exactly what I've done." ✐

NS/ND/C/DWF Wondering Why She Can't Find Someone

MINNEAPOLIS—Susan Stenerud, a divorced, white, non-smoking, non-drinking Christian who has placed "countless" personals ads over the years, wondered aloud Monday why she can't find someone special. "All I want is to find a D/D-free NS/ND/C/SWM who shares my strong morals and doesn't waste his time going to bars and parties," the 32-year-old said. "For some reason, no men seem to respond to that description."

Local Girlfriend Always Wants To Do Stuff

SALEM, OR—Local resident Steven Bertram is "fed up" with girlfriend Alicia Maas' incessant need to do stuff, a visibly frustrated Bertram reported Monday.

Steven Bertram and Alicia Maas in earlier times, perfectly content to be at home and not doing anything.

According to the 31-year-old maintenance technician, Maas, 29, regularly insists that the couple engage in an endless series of activities, things, and events, at various times of the day, despite the fact that Bertram would often prefer not to do such stuff.

"Just yesterday she was going on and on about how much she wanted to see a movie," said Bertram, noting that he had, after repeated requests, taken the demanding Maas to a local cineplex only two months prior. "How many movies does a person need to see in a year? Sometimes I just want to relax."

Though he and Maas have dated for almost two years, Bertram reportedly did not recognize the severity of his girlfriend's near-chronic dependence on getting out of the house and doing stuff until six months ago, when she insisted the two attend a free outdoor concert in their neighborhood. Since that time, Maas has asked an estimated 11 times to be taken to dinner, 17 times to go grocery shopping, and, on 20 separate occasions, has expressed a desire to go on a meandering walk without a fixed destination, purpose, or time limit.

The precise number of incidents, Bertram said, is difficult to determine, as Maas has oftentimes enlisted him in activities without first asking, including initiating seemingly pointless conversations lacking any definitive context or subject matter, as well as making plans with coworkers, family members, friends, old roommates, the people upstairs, and acquaintances Bertram does not know.

In addition, an alarming majority of the activities Maas suggests involve standing up.

"I don't know if I can live like this," Bertram said. "On Saturday I was excited to sit back and watch some TV, and then she

> **"'Alicia is exhibiting all the classic signs of what we call 'active behavior'—an impulse to engage in unnecessary and often prolonged outdoor movement that is most commonly found in females."**

reminds me that [Bertram's best friend] Jeremy [Durst] is having his birthday party, and so next thing you know, I've got to get up, throw some pants on, and hang out with people all night."

"For once I'd like to do what I want to do," Bertram continued. "She always wants to go somewhere or look at something."

Bertram said that for several weeks he attempted to deflect Maas' demands or otherwise dissuade her from pursuing activities outside their one-bedroom

---

"Recently, he has tried to compromise by purchasing an XBox 360 and several multiplayer games for the two to use together, as well as upgrading the couple's Netflix account to allow five DVDs at a time."

---

apartment through a series of complex excuses—including a feigned lower-back injury—but met with little success. Recently, he has tried to compromise by purchasing an XBox 360 and several multiplayer games for the two to use together,

as well as upgrading the couple's Netflix account to allow five DVDs at a time.

Maas' obsession, however, has shown no signs of abating, and on Sunday she volunteered herself and Bertram to walk their neighbors' dog when they go on vacation next week.

"That's three more nights ruined," said Bertram as he toggled between the popular website eBaumsworld.com and a game of online poker. "I could literally be doing anything else, but instead, I'll be walking a dog. I don't need to always be doing stuff, and especially not stuff like that."

According to behavioral psychologist Dr. Michael Greer, though Maas' irrational compulsion for doing things is extreme, it is by no means uncommon.

"Alicia is exhibiting all the classic signs of what we call 'active behavior'—an impulse to engage in unnecessary and often prolonged outdoor movement that is most commonly found in females," Greer said. "Though we cannot be certain, these habits seem to stem from an innate desire to not be doing nothing."

Added Greer, "All available research indicates that this type of unstable behavior is most disturbing when it occurs early in the morning, after 10 p.m., on weekends and perfectly good vacation days, or before one has a chance to finish the third god-damned disc of the second season of *Lost*."

Despite repeated attempts, Maas could not be reached for comment, since she was out at the gym or having coffee with a friend or some shit. ✉

LOVE, SEX, AND OTHER NATURAL DISASTERS

S&M Couple Won't Stop Droning On About Their Fetishes

SANTA FE, NM—According to friends of Jason Roder and Gina Von Poppel, the sexually adventurous couple won't stop droning on about spanking, caning, ball gags, erotic photography, fetish parties, leather, rubber, PVC, latex, whips, floggers, and countless other S&M-related objects and activities.

Gina Von Poppel and Jason Roder.

"When Jason first told me about his and Gina's kinky sex life, I was amazed. I wanted to hear all about it," said Stan Pritchard, Roder's best friend. "But around the 15th time I heard about how great it is to be tied to a chair, I was, like, 'Yeah, I know. The chair. The whip. Being straddled. Got it, thanks.'"

Roder and Von Poppel, who have been dating for almost four years, began experimenting with sadomasochism in July 1999 after buying a few S&M-related items at Santa Fe's Naughty & Nice adult video and novelty store.

"It wasn't until I began experimenting with domination and mistress role-playing that I really discovered myself sexually," Von Poppel has told dozens of people over the years. "It's so liberating to explore the threshold between pleasure and pain."

Meredith Engler, a close friend and former college roommate of Von Poppel's, said she has frequently found herself subjected to hours-long accounts of the couple's S&M exploits.

"Gina and Jason have a pretty open minded group of friends and, at first, we all thought it was cool that they were being so frank about sex," Engler said. "That was our mistake—giving them an opening."

As Roder and Von Poppel delved deeper into sadomasochism, they began dominating nearly every party and social event with endless talk of fetishes, secret fantasies, and forays into bondage and discipline.

> **"'Around the 15th time I heard about how great it is to be tied to a chair, I was like, 'Yeah, I know. The chair. The whip. Being straddled. Got it, thanks.'"**

"When Jason and Gina first told me about their 'secret,' I thought, wow, these people must have one hell of an interesting life," friend Peter Orwitz said. "I couldn't have been more wrong. How many times can a person discuss cock leashes?"

Orwitz said the only thing worse than the couple's lengthy lectures on the positioning benefits of a wall-mounted restraining swing are the long-winded clarifications about the nature of sadomasochism.

"As Jason is constantly pointing out, it's not S&M that they're into: It's BD/SM, which is bondage-domination and sadomasochism,'" Orwitz said. "Apparently, there's a big difference between S&M and B&D. Just ask them. I dare you."

> "'Gina was blathering on and on about domination and I couldn't help but say, 'Well, you're certainly good at conversation domination.' I can't help but wonder if this S&M thing is all a cover-up for their real fetish: talking to people about fetishes.'"

The couple's friends try to avoid topics that might inadvertently lead to discussions of S&M, but the subject always manages to come up.

"It's amazing what will prompt Jason and Gina to talk about sex," Pritchard said. "We had a barbecue last weekend, and I said, 'Pass me the tongs.' So Jason and Gina exchange a knowing look and, before you know it, we're off on an hour-long discussion of how you should put your metal sex toys in the freezer for a few hours before using them."

Roder and Von Poppel have even invited friends to join them in one of their S&M adventures. Thus far, there have been no takers.

"They asked if me and my girlfriend wanted to go with them to Fetish Night at some club called The Dungeon," Pritchard said. "I guess maybe I would have been curious, except I'd already heard every last detail about Fetish Night already. I know about the transgender drag show. I know about the 'secret room' and the 'safe words.' I've heard all about the Saran Wrap woman and the rubber-tubing outfit and Metal-Cage-Around-The-Balls Guy at least five times. So I passed."

After many unsuccessful attempts to subtly communicate her irritation to Roder and Von Poppel, Engler determined that she needed to be more direct.

"Last Friday, Gina was blathering on and on about domination, and I couldn't help but say, 'Well, you're certainly good at conversation domination,'" Engler said. "I can't help but wonder if this S&M thing is all a cover-up for their real fetish: talking to people about fetishes."

Another couple, Sara DeWitt and Ron Crandall, met them at a local bar in May.

"We all had a few drinks and ended up talking about sex almost the entire night," Crandall said. "I remember going home thinking, 'God, these people are nothing like the uptight, boring types I usually hang out with.'"

As the friendship progressed, however, DeWitt and Crandall found that every conversation with the couple eventually turned to S&M.

"The third time we hung out, I started to pick up on the pattern," DeWitt said. "Don't these people have any interests besides vibrating tit clamps? I tried to steer the conversation toward other subjects, but every time I did, they'd start right up with the S&M talk again, telling me not to be so repressed."

Added DeWitt: "For people who aren't uptight or boring, those two are pretty uptight and boring." ✐

Cute Couple On Same Antidepressant

Area Girlfriend Still Hasn't Seen *Apocalypse Now*

AZUSA, CA—In a discovery prompting exasperated forehead-slapping and stunned expressions of incredulity, Mark Tillich learned Monday that girlfriend Brandi Jensen has never even seen *Apocalypse Now*.

Mark Tillich and Brandi Jensen, who, unbelievably, has never seen *Apocalypse Now*, "one of the greatest films of all time."

"You gotta be kiddin' me, Bran!" said Tillich, 21, a senior marketing major at Azusa Pacific University, upon discovering Jensen's ignorance of the 1979 Francis Ford Coppola–directed Vietnam War epic. "It's only, like, arguably the most ambitious anti-war statement in American movie history. Jesus!"

"I cannot believe you've never seen *Apocalypse Now*," he added. "That's insane."

Tillich, who first saw the critically acclaimed film on HBO at age 14 while sleeping over at a friend's house, was particularly distressed by the fact that Jensen had not only never seen the film, but was wholly unfamiliar with its basic premise.

"Hello? Joseph Conrad's *Heart Of Darkness* updated from 19th-century British imperialism in the Congo to a critique of 20th-century U.S. imperialism in Southeast Asia? Hello? Any of this ringing a bell?" Tillich said. "Come on, that's like saying you've never seen *Full Metal Jacket*."

When Jensen replied that she hadn't even heard of *Full Metal Jacket*, Tillich threw up his hands in an "I give up" gesture and stormed out of the room.

"It's not like I don't like movies," Jensen said. "I loved *Notting Hill*, and I'm totally psyched to see *Hanging Up*—I'm the biggest Meg Ryan fan. I even used to have a *When Harry Met Sally* poster in my dorm

> "'It's not that I don't like movies. I loved *Notting Hill*, and I'm totally psyched to see *Hanging Up*—I'm the biggest Meg Ryan fan. I even used to have a *When Harry Met Sally* poster in my dorm room.'"

room. And have you seen *My Best Friend's Wedding*? Julia Roberts and Cameron Diaz are so amazing in it. My all-time favorite, though, has got to be *Beaches*."

Tillich, however, is unimpressed. "He called my movies overwrought, weepy chick dramas lacking in any genuine visceral impact,'" Jensen said. "Well, excuse me for living, Mr. Big Army Guns."

Marlon Brando as Colonel Kurtz, a "mind-blowing" character with whom Jensen is unfamiliar.

Tillich responded to his girlfriend's shocking *Apocalypse Now* revelation by making plans for her to see it that night, claiming that "to deny [her] the pleasure [she] would experience in viewing such a cinematic masterpiece for even one more second would be a crime." Though Jensen declined, telling him she had to study for a test, Tillich persisted, trying to convey to her "the urgency of rectifying this situation as soon as possible."

"After class yesterday, I was hanging out with them, and he wouldn't shut up about it," said Melissa Ayler, Jensen's best friend. "He was like, 'But it's got Robert Duvall's classic turn as the surfing-obsessed helicopter squad leader!' Then he started quoting all these lines from it, saying stuff like, 'Charlie don't surf,' and 'I love the smell of A-bombs in the morning.' At least, I think that's what he said—I've never seen the stupid movie, either."

Tillich's housemate Howie Fuller said that while eating dinner with the couple and several of Jensen's friends, Tillich described in detail the film's climactic scene, in which villagers hack an ox to pieces as The Doors' "The End" plays.

"She was like, 'What's so appealing about an ox getting violently slaughtered? It really doesn't sound like something I'd enjoy, Mark.' And all the girls at the table were like, 'Yeah, that's gross,'" Fuller said. "But that just made him lose it even worse. He started screaming, 'You don't understand! The destruction of the ox parallels

the destruction of Colonel Kurtz! Can't you see that?' It was sad."

According to Tillich, Jensen's failure to see *Apocalypse Now* is her worst cinematic transgression since last October, when the couple was browsing a Blockbuster video store and she casually pointed at the box for Martin Scorsese's *Taxi Driver* and said, "I've seen that. Yuck!" Jensen further outraged Tillich when she rejected such proposed rentals as *A Clockwork Orange*, *Glengarry Glen Ross*, *Wall Street*, and *True Romance*.

Other infamous episodes that have occurred during the couple's 18-month relationship include Tillich's August 1999 insistence that Jensen listen to all of side two of the Velvet Underground's *White Light/White Heat*, his January 1999 failure to talk Jensen into visiting the grave of Philip K. Dick during a Colorado road trip, and his ongoing unsuccessful efforts to get her to read Alan Moore's *Watchmen*, a 1986 postmodern-superhero graphic novel she described as "a comic book about a big

---

"'What in *Apocalypse Now* could possibly be unappealing to a smart, deep, complicated, insteresting 22-year-old woman? It just doesn't add up.'"

---

blue space guy" and that he calls "nothing less than a total, devastating deconstruction of virtually every archetype in the genre's history."

The most frustrating thing, Tillich said, is the fact that Jensen is "exactly my idea of the perfect woman for me," making her ignorance of the seminal film all the harder to fathom and forcing him to call into question, at a profound level, the basic foundation of their relationship and future together.

"You've got to realize, Bran is not just some airhead," Tillich told Fuller over drinks at the Azusa Pacific student union. "She's intelligent, involved, and culturally aware. So how the hell could she not know about Brando and Sheen's classic encounters in Kurtz's depraved jungle fortress? What in *Apocalypse Now* could possibly be unappealing to a smart, deep, complicated, interesting 22-year-old woman? It just doesn't add up."

"I just don't know if I can be seriously committed to somebody who has no interest in seeing *Apocalypse Now*," Tillich continued. "She's just really missing out. I bet she'd love it I could just get her to sit down and watch it." ✐

> # "I just don't know if I can be seriously committed to somebody who has no interest in seeing *Apocalypse Now*. She's just really missing out."

Couple Sneaks Away From Party For A Little Arguing

PHILADELPHIA—After consuming numerous alcoholic beverages and repeatedly locking eyes throughout the night, area couple Tracy Williams and Steve Stills were reportedly so overcome with passion Saturday that they slipped out of Dana Leink's 26th birthday party for a quick 20 minutes of raucous fighting. "There was definitely some electricity between the two of them," said Kelly Brandt, adding that nothing could have stopped the couple from "going at it" for a while. "Tracy and Steve are so intense—I'm not surprised they couldn't keep their hands off each other." According to those in attendance, everyone inside the party could hear the fiery couple's moans as their bodies repeatedly slammed against the wall.

Area Girlfriend, Boyfriend Achieve Perfect Mother-Son Relationship

PORTLAND, OR—After dating for nearly three years, area couple Peter Mazursky and Janet Hyams have finally achieved the perfect semblance of a mother-son relationship, sources close to the pair revealed Monday.

The couple share a moment of familial contentment.

"My little pumpkin would practically be helpless without me," said Hyams, 28, whose role in the adult relationship has slowly transformed from romantic lover to maternal caregiver over time. "I have to supervise almost everything he does, from making sure he gets up in the morning, to reminding him about his doctors' appointments. I even have to pick out his clothes for him when we go shopping together."

Added Hyams, "I don't know how Pete would survive if I weren't around."

The couple—who met in 2005 and have been living together since Mazursky was evicted from his apartment—have not always had it so easy. In the beginning, their interpersonal style still contained many troubling elements of a mature relationship, including periodic moments of independence, mutual equality, and even occasional sexual contact.

> "In the beginning, their interpsonal style still contained many troubling elements of a mature relationship, including period moments of independence, mutual equality, and even occasional sexual contact."

Luckily for the pair, this early period of instability quickly began to break down as arguments over Mazursky's irresponsibility and Hyams' controlling personality gave way to the codependent harmony they now share.

"She takes care of me," said Mazursky,

26, unconsciously looking to Hyams for approval. "With Janet, I never have to worry about stuff like picking up after myself or remembering to brush my teeth before I go to bed. Plus, she always makes all of the big decisions for both of us, which is nice."

Since falling into preprogrammed roles from early childhood, the couple have seen their relationship undergo a number of significant changes. Sexual intercourse, once a favorite and frequent pastime, has

> ## "'My old girlfriend Jessica used to let me eat all the cookies I wanted. We just didn't have the same kind of bond that Janet and I now share.'"

steadily dropped off in regularity, ceasing altogether earlier this month.

"We don't have to be having sex all the time to be happy," said Mazursky, who by this point has entirely sublimated his libido under the weight of his projected need for a maternal protector. "Right now we are focusing on other things, like losing weight. We have a system worked out where I can eat cookies only with Janet's say-so, and if she catches me eating one without permission, she gets to 'ground' me from snacks for a week. It's so great to be able to share that level of intimacy with another person."

"My old girlfriend Jessica used to let me eat all the cookies I wanted," he added. "We just didn't have the same kind of bond that Janet and I now share."

Hyams' maternal duties include always paying the rent for Mazursky and then hounding him to get a job, performing basic household chores to make herself feel useful and needed, and monitoring Mazursky to make sure he doesn't exceed his allotted three hours of video games per day. In return, Mazursky's duties include playing touch football with his friends, giving Hyams someone to subconsciously feel superior to, making the bed after being yelled at to do so, and allowing Hyams to lick her finger and wipe smudges off his face before they go outside.

"When we first met, I knew there was something special about Pete—he was like a big teddy bear you just wanted to tuck into bed," Hyams explained. "That's not to say we don't still have our problems. Sometimes he throws a tantrum when he doesn't want to do the dishes, and I have to discipline him. But when he falls asleep with his head in my lap, it's all worth it."

Mazursky agrees.

"I'm really happy with Janet," he said. "Not every guy's got a girlfriend who calls him from work to make sure he's had lunch. I guess I'm just one lucky kid."

"I really love Mom—I mean, Janet," Mazursky added. ∅

Nation's Boyfriends Dreading 'Free Event In The Park' Season

NISKAYUNA, NY—With summer officially beginning this week, the nation's boyfriends groaned Thursday in anticipation of yet another "Free Event in the Park" season. "Kelly already wants us to go see some Brazilian horn player and these people who use puppets to make fun of politicians. I'm sure they're fine, but we just got AC this summer," said Jason Evans, a boyfriend. "Plus, we go out all the time." A spokesperson for the nation's girlfriends countered that it would be a shame not to take advantage of the tons of cool-sounding cost-free events, which include a craft fair, an outdoor screening of *The Wizard Of Oz*, and the appearance of a modestly successful mid-90s alternative band at the Tulip Festival.

Area Boyfriend Keeps Bringing Up Scrabble Victory

PLYMOUTH, NH—Evan Riedel has made reference to his Sept. 6 Scrabble victory over girlfriend Amy Vanderploeg "about 200 friggin' times" in the days since, Vanderploeg reported Monday.

Amy Vanderploeg with boyfriend Evan Riedel, who is still carrying on about his Sept. 6 Scrabble win.

"Evan will not let that Scrabble game drop," Vanderploeg, 23, said. "Constantly, he'll say stuff like, 'Do you need help reading that magazine article? I know your vocabulary isn't the best, judging from that round of Scrabble we played.' Give it up already, Evan."

The oft-alluded-to match, which took place at Vanderploeg's apartment, was a decisive 382-183 victory for Riedel, who needed less than one hour to dispense with his girlfriend of three years. Upon winning, he performed a brief victory dance and began verbally taunting his vanquished opponent—behavior that has continued unabated nearly two weeks later.

"He works the word 'esteemed' into conversation whenever possible and then says, 'Gee, I really like that word 'esteemed,'" Vanderploeg said. "He was so proud that he'd used up those four e's in one word and used all seven tiles."

Vanderploeg added that by placing "esteemed" across a triple-word-score spot on the board and earning a 50-point bonus for using all his letters, Riedel was able to, in his words, "rack up a sweet 77" on the turn.

In addition to constantly bringing up his best moves, Riedel has relished pointing out errors Vanderploeg made during the game.

> "'He'll say stuff like, 'Do you need help reading that magazine article? I know your vocabulary isn't the best, judging from that round of Scrabble we played.' Give it up already, Evan.'"

"Whenever we see a cat now, he goes, 'C-A-T... Cat!' as a way of making fun of me for putting down such a simple word at one point," Vanderploeg said. "Then he usually says, 'You know where cats like to walk? On the catwalk!' That's because instead of putting down 'cat,' I could've added my 'cat' onto the word 'walk' that was already on the board and gotten a lot more points."

Vanderploeg said she should have anticipated Riedel's post-victory arrogance on the basis of his behavior during the game. "Evan was getting way too into it," she said. "At one point, he got a double-word score and actually screamed, 'Boo-ya!'"

Scrabble game box.

By the midpoint of the game, Riedel had developed an elaborate tile-picking ritual, shaking the bag vigorously before blowing into it and chanting, "Come on, come on, please... gimme the Xs, Js, and Zs!" According to Vanderploeg, such theatrics made it difficult for her to concentrate on the game and contributed to her poor showing.

"There were several times when I put down the first thing I thought of, just to get the stupid thing over with faster," Vanderploeg said. "Every time it was my turn, Evan would lean across the board and stare at me. It started to get really annoying, but whenever I told him to stop, he'd say, 'What's the matter? Can't take the heat?'"

According to noted psychologist Dr. Eli Wasserbaum, Riedel's behavior is rooted in his outsider status during childhood.

"Awkward and ungainly as a boy, Evan never excelled in athletics," Wasserbaum said. "He did, however, find shelter in academia. It is natural, then, that he is most comfortable asserting his male competitive instincts in this arena. His frequent allusion to the Scrabble victory can be likened to a male peacock extending his colorful tail plumage before the female bird. With his constant boasting, Evan is not actually trying to annoy his girlfriend but instead impress her and win her approval."

Riedel has engaged in boardgame-victory braggadocio in the past, carrying on about triumphs in such games as Trivial Pursuit, Balderdash, and Outburst.

"One time, we were playing Scattergories with [longtime couple] Jeff [Weitz] and Kimberly [Alford], and Evan got so bad, I had to cut the game short," Vanderploeg said. "We didn't see them for, like, three months after that."

> **"His frequent allusion to the Scrabble victory can be likened to a male peacock extending his colorful tail plumage before the female bird."**

While Riedel admits to mentioning the Scrabble victory frequently, he denies any wrongdoing.

"I'm just teasing Amy, is all," Riedel said. "Besides, I can't help it if I possess a superior vocabulary and stellar word-formation skills. Cha-ching!" ∅

How Are We Surprising Our Partner?

💜 Opening front door wearing nothing but Vulcan ears

💜 Subpoena taped to Whitman's Sampler box of chocolates

💜 ValenTines™ commemorative fork set

💜 Same appalling body but crammed into skimpy new undergarments

💜 Actual relics of St. Valentine

💜 $30 tip

Boyfriend Ready To Take Relationship To Previous Level

COLUMBIA, SC—Following a romantic three-day getaway to South Carolina's Hilton Head Island, 32-year-old Matthew Sullivan said he is now "more ready than ever" to take his 10-month relationship with girlfriend Carol Moag to the previous level.

Moag and Sullivan are on the brink of a "big leap backward" in their relationship.

"After spending every waking moment with Carol for 72 hours, I know in my heart that I'm prepared to see her face twice, maybe even once a week," said Sullivan, who met Moag, 34, at a friend's New Year's party in January.

Sullivan claimed he has been considering "taking the big leap backward" since Moag suggested last month that the two get a cat. The weekend of uninterrupted intimacy served to erase whatever reservations Sullivan may still have held about the move.

"I know this is a big decision, but I'm ready for it," said Sullivan as he picked up a few DVDs and books he had left at Moag's apartment before she returned home from work. "I've given this a lot of thought, and whenever I imagine giving Carol the keys to her place back, it just feels right."

"I'm so excited about this," he added.

Though Sullivan admitted being initially nervous about Moag's reaction to the sudden announcement, he said he was confident that she will, if not right away, then eventually see that his instincts are correct.

"I'm not sure she'll be ready to take the plunge like this," Sullivan said. "But if I give her plenty of space and lots and lots of time by herself to think it through, she'll realize that we're meant to be together a lot less."

Sullivan said he hoped the couple's new lowered level of commitment will provide them an opportunity to grow as individuals and really make the relationship work for Sullivan.

"It isn't going to be easy, but no one wants this more than I do," said Sullivan, who believes that his clarity at this important juncture is a direct sign of his advanced maturity.

> ## "'When I made the decision to get a lot less serious with Carol, I just felt this sense of peace. I can tell by the look in her eyes—that loving, longing gaze—that I must act now before I miss my chance.'"

"As you get older, you recognize what's really important to you," Sullivan said. "When I made the decision to get a lot less serious with Carol, I just felt this sense of peace. I can tell by the look in her eyes—that loving, longing gaze—that I must act now before I miss my chance."

Sullivan said that he is continually surprised by how "time just flies by" in his relationship with Moag. The 32-year-old said he has a gut sense that if he does not make her aware of his feelings soon, it will be too late.

"What happens now will determine the rest of our future together," said Sullivan, who claimed that he did not want to repeat the mistakes he made in previous long-term relationships. "The last woman I was with [ex-wife Maria Heller], I let this moment pass me by, and I'll always regret it."

"I ended up living with her for two and half years," Sullivan added. *Ø*

> **"'I've given this a lot of thought, and whenever I imagine giving Carol the keys to her place back, it just feels right. I'm so excited about this.'"**

Sex Officials Add New Base Between Second And Third

WASHINGTON, DC—Adolescents across the nation were thrilled by the U.S. Sex Department's announcement Monday that a new base will soon be added. According to Sex Department spokesperson Pat Phelps, the added base will immediately follow second, the touching of breasts, and precede third, the touching of genitals. The new base will involve "the sliding of the hand between the butt cheeks." Sex officials stressed that the base would be considered reached only if the plane of the outer buttocks is broken by the edge of the hand. Baltimore resident Todd Kerr, 15, reported reaching the new base Tuesday with Suzy Hebert, 14, but U.S. sex officials are disputing the claim, asking Kerr to "prove it."

Nation Sickened By Sight Of Happy Young Couple

OAK PARK, IL—Though sharply divided on the war on terror and domestic controversies such as abortion, drugs, and gay marriage, Americans are in almost unanimous agreement over one issue: that Oak Park, IL, couple Dave Petrun and Julie DeSimone are totally sickening.

The happiest goddam couple in the whole world.

"It's like they think they're the first couple to ever fall in love in the history of space and time," said Boston resident Allison Clark, one of millions of people who say they want to shoot themselves in the face after observing the tender relationship between Petrun, 28, and DeSimone, 25, evolve over the last four months.

According to an ABC News–*Washington Post* poll released Monday, a significant majority of Americans believe the couple's persistent displays of affection, which include almost constant hand-holding, mutual giggling, and insufferably coy little kisses, are "fucking ridiculous." An overwhelming eight out of 10 polled said they wished the couple would die, preferably in a fiery automobile accident.

"If I have to see [Petrun] fiddle with [DeSimone's] fingers as they stroll around window shopping, without a care in the world, I swear to God I'm going to punch something," said Savannah, GA, resident Sam Weber, whose reaction has been echoed by a broad cross-section of Americans apparently weary of the couple's brazen public displays. "These two need to face reality, and stop living in this disgusting fantasy world of theirs."

> ## "A significant majority of Americans believe the couple's persistent displays of affection, which include almost constant hand-holding, mutual giggling, and insufferably coy little kisses, are 'fucking ridiculous.'"

Though their initial May 30 joint outing went largely unnoticed, public opinion toward the couple dramatically shifted after it was revealed that DeSimone spooned frozen yogurt into Petrun's mouth during their second date three days later.

By the second week of June, their approval rating dropped below 40 percent in most national polls, after Petrun and DeSimone were spotted wedging their hands into each other's back pockets as they walked through an Oak Park neighborhood. By July, the rating plummeted even further after DeSimone asked Petrun which of her physical attributes he found cutest, and Petrun responded with a detailed list.

"Thirty-six percent of Americans grimaced when Petrun playfully nudged DeSimone for no evident reason last Thursday, and 45 percent emitted a loud, annoyed sigh after Petrun sent flowers to DeSimone's workplace last Tuesday."

"Who are they kidding?" said Rebecca Hillard, a single mother of two in Anchorage, AK. "Once this little honeymoon is over, he's going to cheat on her with an ex-girlfriend and she'll come running to the American people to pick up the pieces. It's so obvious it's stupid."

According to a Sept. 25 Zogby poll, 36 percent of Americans grimaced when Petrun playfully nudged DeSimone for no evident reason last Thursday, and 45 percent emitted a loud, annoyed sigh after Petrun sent flowers to DeSimone's workplace last Tuesday. One in three Americans characterized the way Petrun touched the small of DeSimone's back as he led her into the backseat of a waiting taxi on the evening of Sept. 19 as "completely unnecessary."

"The girl knows how to get into a cab without help," said Adam Burkheimer, a Shreveport, LA, resident and recent divorcé. "I don't get all the constant pawing."

On Wednesday, support lines across the country were flooded with calls complaining of moderate or intense nausea after DeSimone refused, and then eventually accepted, Petrun's hooded sweatshirt during an evening walk.

Online anti-canoodling blogs, such as the popular davejuliebarf.typepad.com, are buzzing with rumors that Petrun and DeSimone broke into a brief, spontaneous slow dance near a Lake Street fountain on Sept. 20.

"Apparently the pussywhipped douchebag smiles when he sees her name on caller ID, too," blogger Jessie Fox said. "If they love each other so goddamn much, why don't they just get married and live happily ever fucking after?"

In recent weeks, elected officials in Nevada, South Dakota, and Virginia passed largely symbolic "Get A Room" ordinances designed to encourage Petrun and DeSimone to make their affectionate displays more private. Conversely, Ococee, FL, banned Petrun and DeSimone from getting a room within its city limits.

While Petrun and DeSimone's behavior does not qualify as a nuisance under any current statutes, the Chicago and San Francisco city councils unanimously passed a joint proclamation encouraging the pair to tone it down.

Read the proclamation in part: "Whereas Dave and Julie are embarking on their first serious relationship, and whereas the odds of it lasting are slim to none, and whereas their ability to make seamless conversation, to instinctively know what the other is thinking, and to relate the story of how the two met when they were randomly seated next to one another on airplane has made nearly 300 million people want to gag, therefore, our cities hereby strongly urge Dave and Julie to really consider breaking up immediately."

Unavailable for comment, Petrun and DeSimone are reportedly making plans to go backpacking across Europe during their six-month anniversary in November, prompting fears that their demonstrativeness could escalate international tensions. ✋

Area Panties In A Bunch

CROSS PLAINS, GA—According to police, a pair of area panties was discovered yesterday all wound up in a bunch and badly in need of some loosening. "Whoever owned these panties," Cross Plains Police Chief Jonathan Norcross said, "obviously needed to relax. Failure to chill out is the number one reason so many panties get bunched in this country each year." Though the panties investigation is still pending, Norcross denied rumors of a connection between yesterday's incident and a pair of Atlanta-area undies discovered last Sunday in a bundle.

New Girlfriend Tests Poorly With Peer Focus Group

RALEIGH, NC—Preliminary data collected Monday from a focus group of friends indicate that new girlfriend Christine Carr is an unsuitable mate for Evan Lindblad.

Members of the focus group discuss Carr (inset).

"I was really excited for everyone to meet Christine," said Lindblad, 25, a graduate student in clinical psychology at North Carolina State University. "I was sure everyone would like her. But now that the numbers are in, I guess I really dropped the ball on this one."

After three weeks of dating, Lindblad held a small party at his home to introduce Carr to a random sampling of his closest friends, ages 22 to 27. Over the course of the evening, Lindblad presented the focus group with a variety of Carr-related queries, ranging from "What do you think of Christine?" to "Is she or isn't she everything I said?"

Lindblad also silently observed focus-group members, making careful note of their spontaneous reactions to Carr.

"At first, everyone was a little shy about speaking up," Lindblad said. "But sometime around 10:45 p.m., when a majority of the focus group was in the kitchen getting beer and Christine was in the other room, everyone really started voicing their opinions. I was right there with the clipboard, taking it all down."

According to Lindblad, Carr scored highest with his five friends from college, with 60 percent of them saying that they "strongly agreed" or "somewhat agreed" with the statement that "Christine seems pretty nice." Carr also fared better with male constituents of the focus group, who were three times less likely to respond disparagingly to the question, "Did you see what she's wearing?"

After tallying Carr's score in the areas of likability, originality, and believability, Lindblad found that his new girlfriend had garnered a meager 23 percent overall approval rating from the group.

> ## "Carr fared better with male constituents of the focus group, who were three times less likely to respond disparagingly to the question, 'Did you see what she's wearing?'"

"It was clear that they simply were not enamored with Christine," Lindblad said. "I'm definitely pulling the brakes on bringing her to Eric Barrowman's Christmas party until I can fully assess this data."

In addition to the low approval rating, 11 focus-group members reported feeling "disinterested" or "bored" when speaking to Carr. Further, while in the kitchen, members compiled a list of her negative qualities they would like to see addressed.

"I did not respond well to that laugh," Lindblad friend and coworker Toni Evers said. "It was way too high. And I would've liked to have seen a little more knowledge about Evan's field of work."

"'I'd heard so many times from Evan how funny Christine was. It was all, 'Christine said this' and 'Christine did that.' Well, at the party, I had a six-minute exchange with her to ascertain her wit quotient, and during that entire time, she didn't make one joke.'"

Carr even scored poorly in areas in which Lindblad expected her to fare well.

"Christine is beautiful, no one can deny that. But feedback indicated that the group wanted to see someone with a 'more mature look,'" Lindblad said. "The midriff-baring shirt actually worked against her in there. Who would have guessed? Well, that's why we do these tests."

By evening's end, a full 84 percent of Lindblad's friends said they agreed with the statement, "Evan can do a lot better."

"I've been close with Evan for several years, and I respect him very much," Evers said. "But if he goes ahead with this relationship, my approval rating of him could drop significantly."

Surprised by Carr's poor showing, Lindblad turned to best friend Jake Hadler for his take on the results. Hadler told Lindblad that his pre-party hyping of Carr, in which he described her as "really funny and incredibly smart," may have backfired.

"I'd heard so many times from Evan how funny Christine was," Hadler said. "It was all, 'Christine said this' and 'Christine did that.' Well, at the party, I had a six-minute exchange with her to ascertain her wit quotient, and during that entire time, she didn't make one joke."

Had expectations not been so high, Carr may have fared better, focus-group participants conceded.

"After the huge build-up, we went in there expecting not merely to be pleased, but blown away," said Lindblad's coworker Glen Delk. "Had Lindblad simply billed Christine as 'great' or 'a really cool girl,' we'd have approached it differently. But he kept saying, 'This girl may be the one,' forcing us to evaluate her potential as a major love interest instead of a minor fling."

Despite the negative reviews, Lindblad is not yet ready to end the relationship.

"I'd hate to kill this so quickly after just one focus group," Lindblad said. "Maybe she can learn a little more about what I'm studying in school. And work on the laugh. That could get the numbers up." *

Jason Statham Beats Wedding Planner To Death In New Romantic Comedy

Girlfriend Changes Man Into Someone She's Not Interested In

CHARLOTTE, NC—After two and a half years of subtle prodding and manipulation, Jill Nickles has finally molded boyfriend Brendan Eiler into the sort of man in whom she's not interested.

Jill Nickles and Brendan Eiler.

"When I first met Brendan, he was a guitarist for [local rock band] The Heavy Petters, and I couldn't take my eyes off him," said Nickles, 28. "I used to go to Tramp's every Thursday night just to watch him play. He wasn't even the most handsome guy in the world, but he just had this mystique, this air of danger about him. He was really exciting. It's too bad he's not like that anymore."

After several months of watching him from the crowd, Nickles finally introduced herself to Eiler after a show in September

1998. They soon began dating.

"Brendan was everything I wanted in a man," Nickles said. "He was unpredictable, smart, and passionate. I knew he wasn't perfect, but he was really fun to be around—which is more than I can say for him now."

Just weeks into the relationship, Nickles began to notice changes.

"It started pretty early," Nickles said. "Instead of being the wild man he'd been, more and more he'd just stay home like a lump, even on nights I told him it was okay if he went out."

Four months to the day after their first date, Nickles moved into Eiler's one-bedroom apartment. The move only accelerated the changes in him.

"Jill and I weren't living together long before she started getting irritated by how small the apartment was," Eiler said. "She was always complaining about how

> **"'Brendan was everything I wanted in a man. He was unpredictable, smart, and passionate. I knew he wasn't perfect, but he was really fun to be around— which is more than I can say for him now.'"**

she didn't have space anymore. Then, she got this idea to get a bigger place, but I couldn't really afford it, since I was just barely scraping by with what I earned bartending at Mickey's. I really liked bartending, and it allowed me flexible hours for band practice and gigs. But, like Jill said, I was 25 now and shouldn't be living hand-to-mouth."

> ## "'All I used to care about was hanging with my friends and having a good time. I guess it's true that the love of a good woman can really change you for the better.'"

At Nickles' urging, Eiler quit his job at Mickey's and landed a position at SFR Solutions, a Charlotte-area web-design firm. The job paid nearly $4,000 a year more than bartending, enabling the couple to move into a larger apartment.

With a full-time job and a live-in girlfriend, Eiler's relationship with his bandmates soon began to deteriorate.

"They kept wanting to play more and more gigs, and I felt like if we wanted to land a record deal, what I needed to do was stay home and write some strong new material," Eiler said. "Even Jill had stopped going to see us because she said she was getting sick of hearing the same songs—and she was our number-one fan. Finally, they said I had to make more time for shows or they'd get a new guitarist. I was like, 'Screw you guys,' and left. Jill pointed out that the band wasn't really going anywhere anyway, and that I was better off in no band at all than one made up of a bunch of unambitious losers."

Upon quitting the band, Eiler's lifestyle changes accelerated. In September 2000, he cut his long mane of hair in an effort to land a promotion to associate design director at SFR Solutions. Nickles also convinced him to become a vegetarian and sell his customized leather jacket to put a down payment on a new Toyota Camry.

"When we first started dating, Jill loved how I looked in that jacket," Eiler said. "But then, a few months later, she said I was getting too old to wear something like that. Plus, it didn't really gibe with my new vegetarian beliefs. So, with Jill's full support, I decided it was time to put my old ways to rest."

Now a self-described homebody, Eiler said he finds his domestic lifestyle "really satisfying."

"If you told me two years ago that I'd be thinking of marriage, a house with a picket fence, and kids, I would have said you were nuts," Eiler said. "All I used to care about was hanging with my friends and having a good time. I guess it's true that the love of a good woman can really change you for the better."

Despite Nickles' success in sculpting Eiler into "husband material," she found her attraction for him beginning to wane.

"The reason I fell so hard for Brendan was that he was totally different from the guys I used to date," Nickles said. "He had beautiful long hair, and he was really smart and cynical. Now he reminds me of my boring ex-boyfriend Kevin, who's an accountant in Raleigh."

Even though Nickles' nights of going out to see The Heavy Petters are long over, she still enjoys going out on occasion.

"A couple of weeks ago, I was at the bar Brendan and I used to go to all the time," Nickles said. "I ran into Rob, the bassist for Brendan's old band and, I have to tell you, he looked really good. We hung out and talked for hours and just had a great time. Drinking and laughing with him really reminded me of the way it used to be with Brendan. I think I'm developing a little crush on Rob." ∅

Longtime Sexual Fantasy Awkwardly Fulfilled

LEXINGTON, KY—The longtime sexual fantasy of Andrew Marcone was awkwardly fulfilled Saturday, when the local record-store clerk participated in a clumsy, embarrassing *ménage à trois* with girlfriend Karen Wagner and her roommate Shelley Peelen. "Well, I finally did it, for what it's worth," said Marcone, 27, following the long-dreamed-of sexual encounter, six minutes into which he ejaculated. "So much for wondering what it would be like, I guess." After achieving orgasm, Marcone spent the next half hour "trying not to get in the way" of his companions.

Voyeur Concerned About Lack Of Sex In Neighbors' Marriage

EDWARDSVILLE, KS—Local Peeping Tom David Sutcliffe expressed concern Monday that next-door neighbors John and Kimberly Hobsbaum's love life may be in jeopardy.

Peeping Tom David Sutcliffe.

"On the surface, John and Kim appear to be the perfect couple," said Sutcliffe, 39, who claimed to know the couple better than most. "They live in a tastefully decorated three-bedroom home, are the proud parents of a beautiful son, and possess all the trappings of modern convenience. But when you take a closer look at their life through the lenses of a powerful set of binoculars, their marriage isn't all it seems."

Sutcliffe said he first suspected that something might be wrong with the Hobsbaums' relationship after seeing Kimberly quietly crying in the shower six months ago.

"I almost didn't notice it at first," Sutcliffe said. "But when I zoomed out on my camcorder, there she was, weeping."

According to Sutcliffe, the rare occasions when Kimberly and John engage in sexual intercourse lack the spontaneity of the early years of their relationship. "There was a time when they, and I, simply couldn't predict when an impulsive love-making session would break out," said Sutcliffe, who admitted that he hasn't needed to move his camouflaged camcorder from its tripod in months. "You don't have to examine hundreds of hours of recorded footage to figure out that sex has become a chore for the Hobsbaums," Sutcliffe said.

"Although it does help."

> "'Maybe Kimberly could greet John one evening in nothing but her red lace teddy. Or, at the very least, she could insist that they have sex with the lights on, adding spontaneity and making my night-vision goggles unnecessary.'"

While Sutcliffe said it would be "unrealistic" to think the couple could rekindle the same passion found in their early days—particularly the "unforgettable" evening of Oct. 12, 1998—he said they can still take steps to recharge their sex life.

"Men are visually stimulated," Sutcliffe said as he dimmed the lights, unbuttoned his pants, and leaned forward to peer through a narrow opening in his window blinds. "Maybe Kimberly could greet John one evening in nothing but her red lace teddy. Or, at the very least, she could insist that they have sex with the lights on, adding spontaneity and making my night-vision goggles unnecessary."

Continued Sutcliffe: "If that doesn't work, perhaps the Hobsbaums could try introducing another person into their bedroom—perhaps that fit, redheaded friend of theirs who sometimes comes over for dinner."

Sutcliffe had dozens of other suggestions, including slower, more sensual foreplay, inventive role-playing based on Victorian themes, experimenting with new sexual positions on their back patio, and, should all else fail, "videotaping their lovemaking sessions."

Sutcliffe warned that couples often don't realize that small gestures like a kiss good-bye in the morning clear of any sight-line obstructions such as tall floor lamps, can make all the difference in the world. "Honestly, I can't remember the last time I

The Hobsbaums.

lip-read John telling Kimberly that he loved her," Sutcliffe said.

"This couple needs to talk about their problems, not ignore them," he went on. "More than anything, they need honest, clear communication, preferably with a lot of sexually explicit verbalizations near an open window within range of my shotgun microphone."

Although the Hobsbaums may have reached a low point in their sex life, Sutcliffe pointed out that this is not an uncommon occurrence among married couples he's observed.

"'More than anything, they need honest, clear communication, preferably with a lot of sexually explicit verbalizations near an open window within range of my shotgun microphone.'"

"I've sat in this chair or crouched in my garage and watched this happen many times before," said Sutcliffe, who asserted that an outsider's perspective is invaluable for recognizing problems in a marriage. "Many couples, like the Menekens directly across the street, or the Stephensons, whose bedroom faces my kitchen, forget that sustaining a loving relationship requires a lot of hard work."

The good news, according to Sutcliffe, is that the Hobsbaums' decreased sex life doesn't seem to be the result of physical illness or inadequacy. "They're clearly still interested in sex," he said. "At least these photos, taken during the day when John was alone in the computer room, seem to indicate this."

Yet Sutcliffe added that, unless the Hobsbaums start mending their relationship soon, he fears one of them might look for affection where Sutcliffe won't be able to closely monitor them.

"I would hate to see something like that happen to such a photogenic couple," he said. ✿

Fuck-Buddy Becomes Fuck-Fiancé

MIAMI, FL—In spite of the explicitly casual nature of their relationship, fuck-buddies Nora Ingersoll and Keith Hetzel are engaged, friend Tom Stipps reported Tuesday. "Keith and Nora have been fooling around for years, but Keith said they were just friends," Stipps said. "I was shocked when Nora showed up wearing a ring." Later that day, the couple reportedly opened a fuck-joint-checking account.

Breakup Hints Misinterpreted as Marriage-Proposal Hints

KNOXVILLE, TN—Amanda Gentry, 25, has misinterpreted longtime boyfriend Wilson Crandall's recent break-up hints—including erratic behavior and strange, cryptic remarks about their future—as marriage-proposal hints.

The excited Gentry and her boyfriend Crandall, who is not about to propose.

"I can tell Wilson is getting ready to pop the question," Gentry said. "The last few weeks, he's been acting so weird. He keeps saying he needs to 'take stock of his life' and 'face some important decisions he's been putting off.' I hear wedding bells!"

Though Crandall, 26, a University of Tennessee law student, rarely articulates his feelings about the state of the couple's three-year relationship, Gentry said his occasional remarks "speak volumes."

"A couple weeks ago, right after sex, Wilson got really odd and quiet, like he wanted to say something but couldn't get it out," Gentry said. "Finally, he told me, 'I think you're a great girl, and I just want you always to be happy.' Isn't that so sweet?"

The post coital exchange went no further, Gentry said, with Crandall telling her only that he needed to talk to her about their future at some point. Two weeks later, the talk has yet to occur.

"He's studying for the bar, but when he's done, he wants to sit down with me," Gentry said. "He says he has something important to say and that I should brace myself. Isn't it obvious? He's finishing law school this May and thinking about settling down. Goin' to the cha-pel..."

> **"'Whenever we talk about Chicago, he goes on and on about how I'd hate the cold weather and the fast pace. He's such a doll to be concerned about my feelings, but doesn't he know I'd follow him anywhere?'"**

Gentry said she hopes Crandall will take her someplace romantic to propose.

"Wilson recently said something about getting away and going somewhere for a week in March," Gentry said. "A few days later, I caught him looking for plane tickets on the Internet. It's weird that he was pricing tickets for around the time of the NCAA Final Four tournament, since I wouldn't think he'd want to miss that. But, obviously, making a commitment to a life partner is so much more important."

Recently, Crandall has been asking Gentry about her career goals, a line of questioning she misread as a sign that he is mapping out their life together.

"He never asked me about social work before, but he's really been encouraging me to invest more of myself into my job," Gentry said. "He thinks fulfillment at work should be a bigger component of my life. Don't worry, Wilson, I have no plans to give up my career to have babies. Yet."

Gentry said Crandall even let slip that he was thinking about moving away from Knoxville after graduating.

"Wilson's been dropping little hints that he might try to get a job back in Chicago, where his parents and sister are," Gentry said. "He's definitely the type of guy who'd want to be close to his family if he was thinking about the long term."

Crandall has not explicitly invited Gentry to accompany him in the event of a move—an omission Gentry attributes to his fears that she may not want to go.

"Whenever we talk about Chicago, he goes on and on about how I'd hate the cold weather and the fast pace," Gentry said. "He's such a doll to be concerned about my feelings, but doesn't he know I'd follow him anywhere?"

Gentry has also misinterpreted Crandall's recent frugality as an effort to save up money for the future.

"It's so cute how he's trying to cut back on expenses," Gentry said. "We never go out to dinner anymore, or the movies, or even the bars. He must be working on one doozy of a rock."

"Wilson's birthday is coming up soon, March 4," Gentry continued. "Maybe he's planning to pop the question then. I can just see him getting down on one knee and saying that I'm what he wants most for his birthday."

Added Gentry: "God, the next few weeks are going to be unforgettable." ∅

Ex-Girlfriend's Last Electric-Bill Check Remains Uncashed In Area Man's Wallet

BALTIMORE—Ten weeks after girlfriend Jessica Schroeder broke up with him and moved out, Richard Bluff, 24, continues to carry the check for her half of their final Baltimore Gas & Electric bill in his wallet. "Jess gave it to me the day she left, and I just couldn't bear to part with it," Bluff said Monday of the check for $75.92. "I know it shouldn't have any sentimental meaning, but, well..." Bluff has also not been able to bring himself to remove Schroeder's Lady Bic disposable razor from his shower.

Badass Engagement Ring Also Tells Time And Temperature

Break-Up Made Easier With Colorful Visual Aids

HUNTINGTON, WV—Stephanie Duquette's break-up with boyfriend Chris Straub was made easier Sunday with an array of colorful charts, graphs, and other visual aids from Copy Express, a Huntington-area copy shop.

Duquette makes a point to her boyfriend using a chart made at Copy Express.

"When Stephanie came in looking for a way to make her dumping of Chris more effective and memorable, I was more than happy to help," said Copy Express assistant manager Debbie Saldana. "Using our state-of-the-art laser printers, film scanners, Canon CLC 1120 color copiers, and top-notch computer software, Stephanie was able to provide Chris with a clear, eye-catching presentation of his failings as a boyfriend."

Duquette, 20, broke up with Straub, her boyfriend of two years, late Sunday evening, using the visual aids to concisely communicate to him just how unhappy she had been during the last six months of their relationship.

"I needed to express my desire to see other people, but I didn't want it to turn into some huge argument about whose fault it was and whether my actions where fair," Duquette said. "I knew Chris was going to have a lot of questions, and that's when I got out this professionally bound report with the peek-through title '10 Reasons Why I Want Out.'"

Duquette also praised Copy Express for its ability to produce the needed visual aids on a deadline.

"Chris and I had agreed we would have the big 'Where is this relationship going?' talk Sunday night after he got back from his guys-only camping weekend," Duquette said. "By Saturday, I was at my wits' end. I

> **"'Using our state-of-the-art laser printers, film scanners, and top-notch computer software, Stephanie was able to provide Chris with a clear, eye-catching presentation of his failings as a boyfriend.'"**

knew I had only one day to come up with something that would really make a big impression, but I had no idea what."

Originally, Duquette had gone to Copy Express to make photocopies of her farewell letter to Straub, which she intended to distribute to the couple's friends so they would understand her side of the story. Upon seeing Duquette attempt to feed the messy, seven-page handwritten letter into the copier's auto-feed slot, however, Saldana intervened.

"I asked Stephanie if that letter wouldn't be more effective if it were organized with bullet points and had a catchy color banner across the top," Saldana said. "Stephanie was excited by the suggestion, so I told her about a whole range of possibilities, from a laminated graph illustrating Chris' declining spending on birthday and anniversary gifts to a spiral-bound, quick-reference booklet of his shortcomings as a lover printed on heavy-stock ivory paper."

One of Duquette's many sharp-looking presentation materials.

600DPI HP DesignJet printer.

"I said, 'See this line graph, Chris?'" Duquette recalled. "'It clearly shows how my interest in you plummeted after I began taking night classes to learn French. These multi-colored lines represent the appeal of some of the other guys in my class. As you can see, the green line representing Steve is a full two inches higher than the blue one representing you.'"

"Chris was definitely impressed by all the great visual aids," Duquette said. "Throughout the entire presentation, he barely said a word."

> # "'These multi-colored lines represent the appeal of some of the other guys in my class. As you can see, the green line representing Steve is a full two inches higher than the blue one representing you.'"

Duquette's major complaints about Straub—including his failure to spend enough time with her, his frequent unemployment, and his steadily increasing weight—were presented to him on attractive, photo-quality color 24"x36" posters printed on Copy Express' brand-new

For all the help she provided, Saldana is modest about her contributions to the successful presentation.

"Most of the ideas were Stephanie's," Saldana said. "I just helped her maximize her results by finding the best way to present the data that she herself had been collecting in her private journal ever since she and Chris started having problems in March."

Straub said he was "blown away" by the Copy Express materials.

"I never realized the great disparity between the frequency and sincerity of Stephanie's expressions of love and those of my own until I saw it laid out in a vibrant, red-and-yellow pie chart," Straub said. "And when I was presented with a glossy, spiral-bound packet detailing all the rude comments I have made about her best friend Paulette over the years, how could I disagree with Stephanie's conclusion that she can do better than me? I was sold." ∅

Bachelorette Party Saved By Actual Firemen

Best Man Has No Idea Why He Was Picked

GREENSBORO, NC—Although he has had a cordial relationship with officemate Karl Harrison for almost two years, Jeff Ashland reported Monday that he has no idea why he was asked to be the best man at Harrison's wedding in June.

Jeff Ashland, the best-man-to-be.

"It's an honor, I suppose," Ashland said from his cubicle at Whitehead Consulting. "I just wish I knew why it fell to me. Karl went to college just down the road, and he's lived in Greensboro for five years or so. He must have met at least a few other guys during all that time, right? But *I'm* the one he chooses to be his right-hand man on the biggest day of his life?"

Harrison asked Ashland to be his best man on March 12, the same day he publicly announced his engagement to his girlfriend of four years, Tracy Newman. Ashland said he had trouble feigning the joy expected of someone assuming such an honor.

"Karl came up to me with this big grin on his face, so I figured his business card was picked out of the fishbowl at the Gumbo Pot again," Ashland said. "But he told me he'd proposed to his girlfriend the night before. As I was congratulating him, trying desperately to remember Tracy's name, he dropped the bomb. He said it'd be 'awesome' if I'd be his best man. At first I thought he was making one of his non-funny jokes, but he was serious."

Ashland said he felt he had no choice but to accept the invitation.

"What could I say?" Ashland asked. 'Sorry, you're just some guy I work with—go look up someone you knew at summer camp'? Seriously, doesn't he know, say, anyone else in the entire world? Doesn't he have a cousin somewhere?"

> **"'What could I say? 'Sorry, you're just some guy I work with—go look up someone you knew at summer camp'? Seriously, doesn't he know, say, anyone else in the entire world? Doesn't he have a cousin somewhere?'"**

Adding to Ashland's misgivings about standing before a crowd in support of Harrison's nuptials is the ever-increasing list of duties the groom has asked the best man to perform.

"Apparently, I'm sort of a ringmaster

for the whole thing," Ashland said, flipping through the Greensboro tuxedo-rental listings. "I knew I had to be the bridesmaid's

> # "'Karl's always talking about how nice it is to have someone as cool as Jeff at the office. God only knows what they're up to all day, but boys will be boys. It's great that Karl and Jeff got so close in so short a time, especially since Karl doesn't make friends easily.'"

date, but now Karl says I'm also in charge of the ushers and shuttling the damn presents around. I really don't need this hassle on top of the wedding-dinner speech."

"My only hope is that the kind of guy who asks a coworker he barely knows to be his best man won't have very high standards," Ashland added.

Ashland said he has been forced to research the speech.

"I've been plying Karl with questions about his courtship, his childhood, and his parents' reaction to the engagement, just to get anything that will give me an inkling of what to say," Ashland said. "And Tracy—who, as best frickin' man, I've finally had the pleasure of meeting—is no help. How can I ask her personal questions about Karl without tipping her off to the fact that I have no idea who he is?"

In spite of Ashland's concern, the bride-to-be has expressed no misgivings about her future husband's best man.

"Karl's always talking about how nice it is to have someone as cool as Jeff at the office," Newman said. "God only knows what they're up to all day, but boys will be boys. It's great that Karl and Jeff got so close in so short a time, especially since Karl doesn't make friends easily."

Harrison had little to say on the subject of his selection criteria for best man.

"It's so nice that Jeff's doing this," Harrison told acquaintances at an after-work get-together, which Ashland, citing a need to shop for black shoes, did not attend. "We're gonna have such a blast at my wedding. And I can't wait to see what he's got planned for the bachelor party. I have no idea what's going to go down, but if I know Jeff like I think I know Jeff, it'll be booze and strippers all the way." *

Groom Getting Cold Feet About Bachelor Party

WESTPORT, MA—Husband-to-be Matthew Reese experienced "second thoughts" Friday, just moments before attending the bachelor party his friends had been planning for months was set to begin. "How do I know I've picked the right stripper?" said Reese, as he mentally prepared himself to take long walk down the aisle of tables in the Scores VIP lounge. "I've been imagining this moment since I was 12, but now I'm worried the lap dances won't live up to my expectations. What if I'm just not ready for this level of irresponsibility?" Reese went on to say he regretted committing to a single topless bar for the rest of his night, but felt that it was too late to change his mind.

Wedding Enjoyed By No One But Bride

NEW ROCHELLE, NY—The lavish, 250-guest wedding of James and Mindy Gallagher, held Sunday at the New Rochelle Country Club, was enjoyed by no one but the bride.

The bride poses with some of the sufferers.

"Today is such a beautiful day," said attendee Chris Barker, a second cousin of the groom, as he watched the newlyweds dance. "I can't believe I'm stuck spending it at this stupid thing when I could be out playing golf."

Barker, who drove four hours from Philadelphia to attend the event, was then dragged off for a table photo with the 14 complete strangers with whom he was seated.

"I'm pretty sure I've set my all-time single-day record for awkward conversations," continued Barker, forcing a smile as a photographer snapped the table picture. "Not that I could hear anything anybody said to me, what with that godawful wedding band blaring 'Old Time Rock 'N' Roll' and 'Love Shack' the whole time."

Like 249 of the 250 in attendance, members of the bridal party expressed a lack of enthusiasm for the $200,000 affair.

"To be honest, I never really liked Mindy all that much," said bridesmaid Ellen Lessing, 24, a college sorority sister of the bride. "I always thought she was kind of a stuck-up bitch. But when she asked me to be in her bridal party—I guess because I'd been her sorority sponsor back in college—I felt obligated to go. We've had almost no contact since graduation, yet I still flew halfway across the country just to be in the wedding of someone I hardly even know."

Compounding Lessing's misery was the "vomit-worthy" purple and teal dress that she and the other bridesmaids were forced to purchase and wear.

"This abomination cost me $675," said Lessing, who has no plans ever to wear the dress again. "I'd be pissed even if it didn't make me look like a walrus."

Other friends had their own reasons for not having a good time. These ranged from jealousy over not being included in the wedding party to unspoken resentment over all the attention heaped on Mindy to the sad realization that Mindy would drift apart from her single friends now that she is married.

"Well, Mindy had a wonderful time, so I guess it was worth it, because this is her special day," said Dr. Carl Lingren, 54, father of the bride. "As for me, I'm still not sure why I blew almost $2,400 on place settings, but Mindy assured me that spending the extra money to have the seating cards foil-embossed would make the day 'truly special.' You'd think flying her three cousins and great aunt in from Sweden would've been enough to make it truly special, but apparently not."

Dr. Lingren then retired to the bar, where he proceeded to drink heavily.

Not even groom James Gallagher enjoyed the reception.

"This is the best day of my life," said Gallagher, reading from an index card in a robotic monotone. "All my life has led up to this magical moment, the day I am bound in eternal matrimony to my sweet Mindy forevermore."

> "'Mindy assured me that spending the extra money to have the seating cards foil-embossed would make the day 'truly special.' You'd think flying her three cousins and great aunt in from Sweden would've been enough to make it truly special, but apparently not.'"

Sources close to the groom say the commitment-phobic Gallagher had been dreading the event since Mindy first brought up the idea of marriage more than a year and a half ago, confiding to close confidants that he was "just doing it to finally shut her up."

Personal-relations expert and noted therapist Dr. Eli Wasserbaum said Gallagher's attitude is far from unusual.

"For men, trepidation about marriage is common," Wasserbaum said. "And a total lack of interest in the details of a wedding reception is more common still, even among those who marry willingly. As for the small handful of grooms who actually enjoy their wedding receptions, I'd say most of them are latently gay."

According to Ira Giraldi, editor of *Wedding Style* magazine, the dread felt by the average wedding guest is understandable.

"Most people don't enjoy weddings—why would they?" Giraldi said. "They have to sit around for long periods making uncomfortable small talk with people they barely know and will probably never see again. They're expected to help offset the great expense of the wedding by purchasing obligatory gifts arbitrarily chosen off some wedding registry—gifts that reflect nothing about the giver. Plus, it generally eats up an entire day, if not a whole weekend, in cases where air travel is involved."

Continued Giraldi: "Worst of all, nobody is ever allowed to openly express these universally held feelings. The rules of social conduct obligate guests to endure the entire experience with a surface patina of strained gaiety, a mask of merrymaking and good cheer that becomes progressively more difficult to maintain as the event drags on."

Despite the boredom of those around her, Mindy had "the most wonderful day ever," bursting into spontaneous tears of joy at several points during the awful-for-everybody-but-her experience.

"I could dance all night," Mindy said. "I wish Jimmy liked to dance more. But I don't care if I'm out on the floor all by myself. This is my day!"

> "'As for the small handful of grooms who actually enjoy their wedding receptions, I'd say most of them are latently gay.'"

The mother of the bride, traditionally the only other person capable of having a good time at a wedding, was not in attendance, as she died three years ago in a gruesome motorboat accident. Ø

Area Woman Marries Into Health Insurance

SAN FRANCISCO—The romantic motives of local woman Janet Debois, 28, came under scrutiny Sunday following accusations that she had only married Vince Davidson, 31, for his generous health insurance policy. "She wasn't even into Vince until he started flashing his Blue Cross/Blue Shield card around," said Carly Platt, a longtime acquaintance who speculated Debois might one day leave her new husband for an older man with a smaller co-pay. "You could just see the wheels turning in her head once she found out his dental plan covered twice-annual cleanings. Then it was a sprint to the altar." Sources close to Davidson confirmed that he is only getting married so he can use his wife as a tax write-off.

New-Versus-Old Electric-Slide Confusion Blamed In Wedding-Reception Pileup

MALDEN, MA—Twelve wedding guests were critically injured Saturday night in a dance-floor pileup blamed on new-versus-old Electric Slide confusion. "The DJ called for the Electric Slide without specifying which, and when the 'old' Sliders slid to the right, they collided violently with the stationary, hip-shaking 'new' Sliders," paramedic Laura Denison said. "By the fifth bar, the dance floor was a gruesome tangle of bodies." In the wake of the tragedy, the American Association of Disc Jockeys released a statement urging all DJs to specify which Electric Slide they are calling for at any future weddings, retirement parties, and bar mitzvahs.

Newlyweds Regret Saving Sex For Marriage

WETUMKA, OK—Two weeks after their Feb. 1 wedding, Matt and Liz Kuchen, both 32, regret remaining virgins until marriage. "Why the hell did I wait?" Liz said Tuesday. "I could've been having mind-blowing sex with dozens of guys these last 15 years, and instead I spent them making little uptight speeches about how it'll be more special if I hold out." Matt agreed, saying, "Stacy Pratt totally would've done me. Oh, man."

Mattress King Selects Wife From Small Wisconsin Village

OSHKOSH, WI—Joyous tidings were trumpeted throughout the hamlets of central Wisconsin this week after 43-year-old Mattress King James Koepke III, Lord and Master of a vast bed and box-spring empire, selected Beth Lowery, a buxom, flaxen haired maiden from the small village of Waukau, to be his bride.

The Mattress King, as seen in one of his recent televised decrees.

The 36-year-old queen to-be, red of cheek and unmarred by pocks or the great widening of the hindquarters endemic to females of the region, reportedly accepted the king's matrimonial offer without hesitation. The new queen will reign alongside the noble bedroom furnishings monarch, and together they shall rule the mattress kingdom, which spreads across four convenient locations in the Fox River valley.

Following the royal proclamation, the Mattress King and his retinue reportedly celebrated with great relish amongst the citizenry at Tinker's Pub, where Wild Turkey and Miller High Life did freely flow until the early morning hours.

"I'm real happy for [King] Jimmy," said James' most trusted consul since high school, Sir Louis of Wilkinson. "This new one seems like a great gal. All's I gotta say is, it's about time!"

James III—the territory's unchallenged sovereign of discount prices on Sealy, Serta, King Koil, and Tempur-Pedic mattresses since his father, James II, became too enfeebled to run the empire in 1999—has been in search of a suitable queen ever since his last bride, Linda, the Great Bitch of Pewaukee, absconded in the night with a lowborn scoundrel from whom she was taking skiing lessons.

> "The new queen will reign alongside the noble bedroom furnishings monarch, and together they shall rule the mattress kingdom, which spreads across four convenient locations in the Fox River valley."

Though she was banished from James' sprawling split-level Oshkosh palace in 2002, the former queen was able to empty his vast coffers by half, leaving the Mattress King much embittered by romantic conquest for many years.

Sources close to the king said that he remained most dubious about his prospects of ever again finding true love until he was instantly smitten by the fair and reasonably chaste Beth of Waukau, a common serving wench at a local Applebee's.

In his great languishing for his beloved, the Mattress King reportedly could not rest his mighty head in slumber for nigh a fortnight, and supped at the simple chain tavern every day for a month, walking amongst his subjects as one of their own. At last, no longer able to contain his desire, His Highness summoned the courage to request that he be permitted to court her in the customary manner with an evening of bowling.

Though he cared for her deeply, King James at first did hide his noble birthright from Lowery, afraid that his lady love was indeed one of a roving pack of money grubbing whores that had befallen the area.

"I think Jimmy didn't tell her who he was because he got burned so many times in the past," said Kyle Osterberg, trusted ward of the king's fiefdom in Appleton's Fox River Mall. "He wanted Beth to love him for who he is as a person."

According to sources, the dirty-flaxen-haired Lowery finally discovered the king's true identity after seeing him in all his regal dress on a printed edict on the back of the Oshkosh Northwestern newspaper. In the full-color announcement, His Majesty declared himself insane due to the unheard-of discounts he was offering on all Simmons mattresses throughout his kingdom.

Soon after, the Mattress King asked for her hand, paying a handsome tribute to her parents in the form of a 25-percent lifetime discount at any of the franchises under his purview.

"Jimmy is such a great guy, and so much better than the other jerks Beth was always dragging home," said Melinda

The Queen-To-Be.

Lowery, the future Mattress Queen's mother, clearly still in awe of her daughter's unimaginable providence. "And [the queen's father] Clark [Lowery] and I just love our new mattress set."

Though the benefits of mattress royalty will be many, the new queen will not be without her sacred duties. From the day their union is formed, Lowery will be at her husband's side in the back office of the North Main Street location, where her most important charge will be balancing the royal checkbook, because, according to the king's decree, "she's got a great head for numbers."

The Mattress King and his betrothed will reportedly be wed this May, with a lavish reception for the local peasantry to be held at the Delmar Party House. Sources said that no expense will be spared for the wedding feast, where local delicacies will abound, including innumerable hot wings from Purcell's Bar & Grille.

The queen is expected to produce an heir to the throne in six and a half months. ✑

Kiss With Wife Pretty Good

DENTON, TX— Forty one year-old printer repairman and husband Nils Holzer was shocked by the quality of a kiss he shared with his wife before going to work last Tuesday. The kiss, which experts estimate to be the couple's 4,287th, lasted eight seconds longer than their previous and featured more animation on the part of both participants. "Well, whadaya know?" Holzer said, "That was pretty all right. She even moved her hands around on my back. I forgot about that." Holzer thought about the kiss for most of the day, and was at press time considering doing something nice for her, like buying some of those daisies she likes.

Marriage Handled Amicably

DAVENPORT, IA—Despite the bitter emotional toll it has taken on them, Beth and David Harrigan expressed relief Tuesday that they have been able to handle their 11-year marriage so amicably.

According to Beth, while it's clear that they will never fully reconcile their differences, she and David are doing their best in a bad situation.

"It can get pretty tense when the two of us have to be in the same room together, and the holidays are definitely awkward," Beth said. "But overall, I think we've managed to be really civil throughout the whole ordeal."

"Marriage is obviously a terrible, terrible thing, but it doesn't mean we have to be at each other's throats," Beth added.

The Harrigans also maintained that, while they may no longer be in love, they still both have a great deal of respect for each other.

The couple's biggest concern has reportedly been their children, Simon, 7, and Laura, 9. Beth said that while she and David realized they could never completely protect the kids from the damaging effects of their continued union, they were doing their best to honestly answer any questions that come up.

"The marriage has been really hard on the kids, but we're making sure they know it's not their fault that it's like this," said Beth, adding that she tries not to bad-mouth David within earshot of her son and daughter. "Children are very perceptive—they can always tell when something's wrong—so we decided not to keep anything from them. It's not like we're ever going to be a happily married couple again, but at least we can try to make it as painless as possible for them."

David said that the marriage has been challenging for him personally, but it has also afforded him the opportunity to grow. According to the self-employed accountant, he now spends most of his time in his home office in the basement, an

Beth and Dave Harrigan say they see no reason why their marriage can't be as painless and civil as possible.

> ## "'The marriage has been really hard on the kids, but we're making sure they know it's not their fault it's like this.'"

arrangement that still allows him to see his children frequently.

"In some ways, the whole thing has actually been good for me," David said. "It was such a huge relief when Beth and I could finally sit down and say, 'Look, this thing isn't working, but what are you gonna do? Life goes on.'"

"Now I just have to build up the courage to start seeing other people," David continued.

Though things between the couple remain strained, David and Beth both said they look forward to moving past the unpleasant experience as soon as the other dies. *Ø*

Attractive Woman, Wealthy Man Somehow Making It Work

GREENWICH, CT—Despite their disparate backgrounds, lack of mutual interests, and seemingly insurmountable gap in age, former Miss Kentucky finalist Amber Williams, 26, and multimillionaire real estate mogul Chester R. Williams II, 61, told reporters Monday that they somehow continue to make their marriage work. "The moment I saw her, I knew I wanted to marry her," said Chester Williams, adding that the couple's relationship has inexplicably persevered despite the fact that they usually see each other only one or two nights a week. "Amber said she had always been waiting for somebody like me to come along and sweep her off her feet. I suppose she was exactly what I was looking for, too." Sources close to the pair confirmed that it is almost as if the two were "made for each other."

Amazon.com Recommendations Understand Area Woman Better Than Husband

SANDUSKY, OH—Area resident Pamela Meyers was delighted to receive yet another thoughtful CD recommendation from Amazon.com Friday, confirming that the online retail giant has a more thorough, individualized, and nuanced understanding of her taste than the man who occasionally claims to love her, husband Dean Meyers.

"To come home from a long day at work and see the message about the new Norah Jones album waiting for me, it just made my week," said Meyers, 36, who claimed she was touched that the company paid such attention to her. "It feels nice to be noticed once in a while, you know?"

Amazon, which has been tracking Meyers' purchases since she first used the site to order *Football For Dummies* in preparation for attending the 2004 Citrus Bowl as part of her husband's 10th wedding anniversary plans, has shown impressive accuracy at recommending books, movies, music, and even clothing that perfectly match Meyers' tastes. While the powerful algorithms that power Amazon's recommendations generator do not have the advantage of being able to observe Meyers' body language, verbal intonation, or current personal possessions, they have nonetheless proven more effective than Dean, who bases his gift-giving choices primarily on what is needed around the house, what

he would like to own, and, most notably, what objects are nearby.

"I don't know how Amazon picked up on my growing interest in world music so quickly, but I absolutely love this traditional Celtic CD," Meyers said. "I like it so much more than that Keith Urban thing Dean got me. I'm really not sure what made him think I like country music."

Meyers said she was especially moved that the online merchant remembered that she had once purchased an Ian McEwan book, and immediately reminded her when the author released a new novel. Moreover, despite having had only 37 hours of direct interaction with Meyers, Amazon was still able to detect her strong interest in actor Paul Giamatti, unlike husband Dean, who often teases Meyers about her nonexistent crush on Tom Cruise.

Meyers said she was pleasantly surprised to receive three e-mails from Amazon today alone.

Meyers said that her husband, whose gift choices have never reflected any outward recognition of her desire to learn Spanish, nor of the fact that she looks terrible in orange, rarely, if ever, communicates with Meyers while away on any of his frequent business trips.

"I was having some tea from that Nebraska Cornhuskers mug Dean got me for Valentine's Day, when a little e-mail from Amazon popped up out of the blue," Meyers said. "Just completely out of the blue."

"It was nice to know that on my birthday, someone or something was out there thinking about me, and what boxed sets I wanted," she added.

"'I don't know how Amazon picked up on my growing interest in world music so quickly, but I absolutely love this traditional Celtic CD. I like it so much more than that Keith Urban thing Dean got me. I'm really not sure what made him think I like country music.'"

Though "it could only be a coincidence," Meyers admitted that she became emotional during a recent "bad day" when the site recommended the DVD *The Umbrellas Of Cherbourg*. "Dean and I saw it on one of our first dates, and I remember it being such a great night not just for the movie, but how everything felt so natural, how we seemed to be on the same wavelength," Meyers said. "It was the first time I thought, 'Yes. This is the one.'"

While Amazon is almost always accurate, the company does occasionally make a gift recommendation that does not

suit her tastes, such as a recent suggestion of camping gear and an all-weather backpack. Still, Meyers lauded Amazon's attempts at spontaneity.

"At least it's trying," said Meyers, whose husband will once again surprise her with their fourth romantic getaway to his hometown of Kenton, DE, sometime in March. "And maybe I would like camping if I ever tried it. Amazon's usually right about these things."

Meyers, who has spent the past 15 years with a man who still believes she enjoys attending car shows, said she has kept her Amazon recommendation e-mails a secret from her husband so as not to corrupt the "deep and unstated understanding" between her and the popular website.

"Sure, I could send him the link to my Wish List, but that really defeats the purpose of gifts, as far as I'm concerned," Meyers said.

For his part, Dean has promised to make a concerted effort to pay closer attention to his wife's habits in order to choose

"'It was nice to know that on my birthday, someone or something was out there thinking about me and what boxed sets I wanted.'"

more appropriate and tasteful gifts. He said that she will be "pleasantly surprised" with his new strategy, enrolling her for the next three years in the Oprah Book Club.

"I know she's really into *The View*, so I just figured this would be perfect," Dean Meyers said. "And I know she'll love taking moonlight drives on our new riding mower together, too." ✍

Frustration With Husband Taken Out On Soap Scum

FAYETTEVILLE, AR—Local homemaker Darlene Ernst, 37, expressed her frustration with her husband, Dean, on Tuesday by vigorously scouring the stubborn soap scum from her bathtub's surface. "A clean bathroom takes a lot of work, and maybe I'm not always in the mood to do it, but I do it anyway because it's the right thing," said Ernst, whose spouse's emotional unavailability is similarly responsible for her home's dust-free mini-blinds and spotless attic. "I will not let this soap scum ruin my life." Sources report that Ernst treated herself to a new Clorox ReadyMop over the weekend after hearing from neighbors that her husband was seen with another woman.

Husband Still Faithful After 42 Years Of Trying To Cheat

SARASOTA, FL—Through the ups and downs of raising four children, years of financial hardship, and all the stresses and turmoil of daily life, claims adjuster Arnold Schneider has stayed true to his wife of 42 years, despite his most determined efforts to engage in sexual intercourse outside of wedlock.

"I could never be unfaithful to Helen," said the 63-year-old Schneider, who over the past four decades has unsuccessfully attempted extramarital relations with dozens of friends, acquaintances, work colleagues, and random strangers. "Sure, there have been some tough times, and we all have moments of doubt, but Helen is the woman I love."

Added the man who has attempted to trade in his wife for the first willing female participant hundreds of times over, "Even I'm amazed by that sometimes."

According to sources close to the couple, Schneider has remained grudgingly loyal and devoted to his wife from the very beginning, failing time and again to cheat on his unsuspecting bride during their honeymoon together in Acapulco.

"I'll never forget Mexico—the beaches, the stars, the amazing food and people," said Schneider, who, as his new wife lay sound asleep in bed, would routinely sneak out of their hotel room and try in vain to hit on the young cocktail waitress tending the bar downstairs. "It was perfect. Pretty much almost perfect."

Over the next decade, Schneider remained faithful to his wife by default, repeatedly coming up short during his

Schneider and the woman who would have almost certainly left him had he not failed at infidelity.

regular jaunts to singles clubs, at neighborhood key parties, and through the general freewheeling sexual bacchanalia of the 1970s.

> ## "Whether he was being stood up by the woman who answered his personals ad, or unsuccessfully attempting to persuade his wife's more attractive sister to visit a clothing-optional spa, Schneider said that what mattered most was that he never once wavered."

"It was a crazy time and a lot of my friends didn't think twice when it came to breaking the sacred bonds of marriage," said Schneider, who despite throwing himself at any available woman in his presence, completely failed to capitalize on his adulterous tendencies. "But not me. No sir."

"Not even once," Schneider added with a heavy sigh.

Despite being left with no choice but to stay committed to his marriage, the reluctant husband and father admitted that being loyal wasn't always so easy. With a growing family and increased tension at work, Schneider said there were times when he could have taken comfort in the arms of another.

"Yes, there were moments when I found myself on the verge of the unthinkable," said Schneider, who once drove 300 miles to meet an old girlfriend from high school, only to be flatly rejected by the woman and have coffee thrown in his face. "Still, for one reason or another, I just couldn't go through with it. And when it was all over, I could look myself in the mirror and say, 'Forty-two years, and you've never been with anyone besides your wife.' Forty-two goddamn years."

Schneider acknowledged that even in less troubling times he occasionally felt restless after four decades with the same partner. But whether he was being stood up by the woman who answered his personals ad, or unsuccessfully attempting to persuade his wife's more attractive sister to visit a clothing-optional spa, Schneider said that what mattered most was that he never once wavered.

"Heck, I've got eyes, and I'll notice a pretty face just like anyone else," said Schneider, who at press time was still hoping to hear from a pancake-house waitress he had given his business card to three weeks earlier. "But what can I say? There's an ultimate line Arnold Schneider just can't cross. I'm not even sure I'd know how, to tell you the truth."

For her part, Helen Schneider said she had no doubt that, through it all, her husband has always been faithful.

"Maybe I'm naïve," Helen said, "but I've known this man most of my life, and I just can't imagine him cheating on me. Honestly, Arnie's my little saint." *∅*

Storybook Romance Leads To In-Flight-Magazine Marriage

MORRISTOWN, NJ—A romance straight out of a storybook has led to a marriage straight out of an in-flight magazine, it was reported Monday. "Matthew and Lorraine DeRola, who wed one year ago after the kind of magical courtship you read about in fairytales, now live the kind of lives that are as exciting as an in-flight magazine, industry trade journal, or dental-health brochure," said Larry Garber, who lives next door to the utterly-bored-with-each-other DeRolas.

My Man's Intuition Tells Me My Neighbor Wants To Sleep With Me

I don't even know what you'd call it—a sixth sense, a little voice, a certain gut feeling—but every man has a special, indefinable intuition about the unspoken matters of the heart. I first noticed mine when I was a teenager. Sometimes it's vague, other times it's a sensation you feel right in your core, but whatever it is, I always pay it heed, and it's never steered me wrong.

by Edward Jonas

And ever since that little blond hottie moved in down the street, my man's intuition's been going off like crazy. See, most people aren't in tune enough with their intuition to see that my neighbor, with her tight body and teasing eyes, is desperate to take a ride on the Jonas pony. After all, as a young, energetic yoga instructor married to some rich, handsome guy who does something in business or stocks or whatever, she seems to have it all. I might not be the best-looking guy on the block, but I've been around it a few times, and I know when I'm getting vibed. Particularly when they are sex vibes.

My man's intuition is telling me that she wants to sleep with me, and it's telling me she wants it bad. Real bad.

Male intuition is hard to explain. All men have it, but most either don't understand it or never effectively develop it. To me, it's absolutely indispensable. How else would I pick up on life's silent little cues? Like with this new neighbor: Every time I see her from afar, I get this twinge that tells me she wants nothing more than for me to slip in through the back door to find her wearing bike shorts, a tank top, and pigtails, and give it to her long and hard while her husband is at work.

> **"I might not be the best-looking guy on the block, but I've been around it a few times, and I know when I'm getting vibed. Particularly when they are sex vibes."**

Even I found it hard to believe at first. But about two weeks after they moved in, I ran into her at the grocery store, and as I was introducing myself, my male intuition started pumping like mad. I don't even remember what we were talking about, but after two minutes I knew that there was a connection. A sex connection. I could probably have taken her right there in the paper-towel aisle, but my male intuition said it wasn't the time or place. So I played it cool.

The signals just kept coming, though. Whenever she saw me outside working, she'd wave and sometimes say, "Hey, Ed." Then I noticed that she'd walk in front of the dining room window every night, knowing full well that it was directly across from my house. And every night at around the same time, she'd wash the dishes in one of those teeny shirts she likes to wear. I would just sit in my completely darkened living room, watching her jiggle and sway as she scrubbed those pans. Damn, does my male intuition go crazy when she's doing stuff like that.

My friend Deborah from work thinks that I'm deluding myself. She says that a happily married woman like that would never want to get with a guy like me. What you have to remember, though, is that Deborah, like all women, just doesn't get it. Without a man's intuition, there's no way she could sense what's really going on here. Besides, she's probably just jealous, because my intuition says Deborah totally wants me even though she says she's a lesbian. I can see how that would make her confused.

Yeah, my male intuition tells me that it won't be long before something happens between this neighbor and me. Something sexual. All I have to do is pay close

> "She's probably just jealous, because my intuition says Deborah totally wants me even though she says she's a lesbian. I can see how that would make her confused."

attention and wait for her sign that she's ready. It could be something as small as her forgetting to lock the bathroom door while she's showering. Whenever it is, believe me, I'll be there. And my male intuition tells me that she's going to love it. ✐

Best Thing That Ever Happened To Area Man Yelling At Him About His Socks

MINNEAPOLIS—Joseph Collins, 38, who is perhaps the luckiest man alive and who certainly doesn't deserve the wonderful woman who showed him what it was like to be happy, was chastised by the love of his life for sock-related reasons Thursday. "Look at the holes in these toes," sighed Collins' perfect match, who found him when he was adrift in his late 20s and brought joy and tenderness into his life. "And these are your good SmartWools. You have to treat your things right, honey. Are you listening to me?" At press time, Shelly Collins' knight in shining armor was spilling cookie crumbs all over the couch she had just cleaned.

Gay Marriage

Last week, the Massachusetts high court sanctioned same-sex marriages in that state. What do *you* think?

Karl Collins
Mechanical Engineer

"Same-sex unions will only serve to weaken the institution of marriage for the rest of us. My wife and I can barely stand each other as it is."

Joe Perez
Waiter

"How will they decide who's going to wear the wedding dress?! Whoa! Sorry for being so 'politically incorrect'!"

Frances Evans
Producer

"What's the big deal? It's legal now. My sister's married to a gay guy and everyone knows it."

Walter Hill
Systems Analyst

"Great. Just when I finally get my mother to accept that I'm gay, she has a whole new thing to nag me about: getting married."

Jerry Turner
Musician

"Some fag better not try marrying me. These days, you fuck a guy one time and he pulls out a ring."

Diane Morris
Counselor

"As an overweight, emotionally needy fag hag, I strongly oppose all gay marriage legislation."

Lack Of Second Car Preserves Marriage

CHICKASAW, AL—Though they've weathered some rocky times during their five years of marriage, Dale and Sheila Hefko have managed to stay together. The couple's secret? Their lack of a second car.

Dale and Sheila Hefko and the lone car that holds them together.

"This marriage hasn't exactly worked out like I expected, but we're determined to stick it out," he said. "At least until I get my own car so I can still get around."

"So long as we've only got one car between us," Dale continued, "ain't nobody's going nowhere."

Sheila expressed a similar determination to preserve their sacred union, held together by the used 1990 Ford Escort she and Dale bought for $3,100 in 1995.

"Last Friday, when I found out about Dale and [neighbor] Rhonda [Geilstead], I was gonna kick him out of the house for good," Sheila said. "But I knew he'd take off in the car if I did, and I had to go to the dentist in Mobile on Saturday. I wasn't about to wait two months for a new appointment, so I didn't even bring the Rhonda thing up."

Despite their difficulties, the Hefkos realize that divorce is not something to be taken lightly.

"Even if the court says I get the car,"

Sheila said, "I can't take it, because then he don't have no way to get to work, and he gets fired and I don't get child support."

Also factoring into the one-car couple's decision to stay together are their children, Jesse, 4, and Naomi, 1.

"If it weren't for the kids, maybe we wouldn't still be married," Sheila said. "But as it is, I need to get them to the babysitter's and the doctor, and I've got to get to the Piggly Wiggly in Prichard for baby food and diapers. Take all that away, and I'm doing a whole lot less driving."

> "'If it weren't for the kids, maybe we wouldn't still be married. But as it is, I need to get them to the babysitter's and the doctor, and I've got ot get to the Piggly Wiggly in Prichard for baby food and diapers.'"

The car is also needed to transport Dale and Sheila to their respective jobs, as well as to get Dale to his monthly meeting with his parole officer. Sheila described a typical day: "At around 8 a.m., I drop Jesse off at Kidcare, then I take Naomi over to one of my friends, usually Bobbie or Angie, because Kidcare won't take Naomi until

> **"'When you're buying a car, you've got to think of things in terms of the long run. When you sign your name on that title, that car's yours, for better or for worse.'"**

she's 2. Then I wake up Dale, and he drops me off at my waitressing job at the Toot Toot Steak House, then he heads off to the screen-door factory for second shift."

Surprisingly, it was Dale and Sheila's mutual need for a roommate, not a car, that brought them together.

"When I dropped out of high school, my mom kicked me out of the house, so I was just sleeping on people's couches until I could find a place," Sheila said. "Then, when I started messing around with Dale, he said he'd dump his girlfriend if I moved in and picked up her rent. After a few months I got pregnant, so we got married."

Five years later, the pair is still together.

"It's damn near impossible to find a cheap car that isn't gonna end up costing more to fix than what you paid for it," said Dale, who regularly scans the classified ads and visits used-car lots. "See, when you're buying a car, you've got to think of things in terms of the long run. When you sign your name on that title, that car's yours, for better or for worse." ∅

Area Woman Not Yelling At You, She's Just Saying

JACKSONVILLE, FL—Area resident Roberta Pearle clarified Monday that, while it may look like she is yelling at you, she is actually just saying. "I'm not yelling at you," Pearle explained. "I'm just saying. You know, so you'll know." Pearle then loudly reiterated that she is not yelling. "I'm not," she said.

Easy Wife Gives It Up On First Date Night

OMAHA, NE—Local man James Carlson totally got some Friday night when his wife, Shelly, "went all the way" after just one date night, the lucky husband reported. "I figured it'd be at least three date nights before she gave it up, but all it took was a modest dinner and a few glasses of wine, and she went straight home with me, no questions asked," Carlson said of his wife of eight years, with whom he has three children, James Jr., 7, Wendy, 5, and Sandy, 3. "After we paid the babysitter and brushed our teeth, she couldn't keep her hands off me." Carlson hopes to continue date-nighting his wife for the foreseeable future, seeing as she is such an easy lay.

Red-Lace Nightie Portends Another Excruciating Night For Closeted Husband

CLARKSTON, GA—A red-lace nightgown, barely covering area resident Amanda Yetter's body, sent waves of dread through husband and closeted homosexual Eric Yetter Friday.

Closeted homosexual Eric Yetter and wife, Amanda.

"I was coming home late from a long, tiring day at the office, and Amanda met me at the door wearing that red thing," said Yetter, 36, referring to the size-large, satin-trimmed, babydoll-style nightgown with matching ruffled thong bikini Amanda recently purchased at Victoria's Secret. "I immediately thought, 'Oh, God, here we go again.'"

Yetter, who has yet to admit his homosexual desires to himself, much less his wife, returned home at 10 p.m. expecting Amanda to be asleep.

"When I pulled in the driveway, all the lights were all off, so I figured I'd be able to just relax and watch some TV," Yetter said. "But as it turned out, Amanda was waiting for me with the whole house lit up with candles and vanilla incense."

Upon seeing his wife in the nightie, Yetter feared that the situation would lead to intercourse, which until that point he had managed to avoid for a record seven weeks. Panicked, he began searching for an excuse.

"As Amanda unbuttoned my shirt, I tried to tell her that we'd wake up Eric Jr., but she said Grandma took him for the night so that we could finally spend some time alone," Yetter said. "Then I told her that I had to get up early to cut the grass, but she reminded me that the mower was broken. That's when I knew there was no way out."

> "'It'd be nice if he enjoyed it more, but you know how men are. When you finally talk them into it, they just want to get in there, shut their eyes tight, and get it over with as quickly as possible.'"

Yetter was led into the bedroom, where playing on the stereo was the CD compilation *Pure Romance*, an album he associates with a particularly unbearable Jan. 6 encounter with his wife involving mutual oral sex. After being instructed to kiss his wife all over, Yetter was then subjected to 23 minutes of marital relations.

"Amanda complains that we don't have sex often enough, but she has to understand that I have a very high-pressure job," Yetter said. "And then there's church, which we're very involved with."

Because of Yetter's strong Catholic faith, the couple abstained from sex until after their June 1995 wedding, an event that was originally scheduled for May 1993 but was delayed numerous times due to "extenuating circumstances."

Amanda said that, overall, she is satisfied with her sex life.

The nightie.

"I have to admit, it isn't exactly everything I've ever wanted, but it's normal for a couple's love life to fall off a bit as time goes by," she said. "Still, I just can't help but wish it was more like it was when we first got married. We were pretty crazy that first day or two!"

In addition to the infrequency of their coupling, Amanda expressed disappointment over her husband's habit of having a few drinks to "loosen up" to the point of inebriation before intercourse, as well as his tendency to face away from her during the act itself.

> # "'I just can't help but wish it was more like it was when we first got married. We were pretty crazy that first day or two!'"

"It'd be nice if he enjoyed it more, but you know how men are," Amanda said. "When you finally talk them into it, they just want to get in there, shut their eyes tight, and get it over with as quickly as possible."

Added Amanda: "I'm hoping, though, that if I can be more creative in the romance department, I can spice things up a bit. Maybe then, Eric won't spend so much time in his study with the door locked."

With Friday's coital duties behind him, Yetter is now focusing on the couple's June 11 anniversary.

"I hope Amanda doesn't expect us to go someplace romantic for the weekend," Yetter said. "A dinner out would be okay, but some secluded little bed-and-breakfast by the sea would be way too much. Amanda should know that sort of thing doesn't interest me." *∅*

Relationship Tips

Many couples find their relationships stuck in a rut after they've been together for a while. Here are some ways to re-kindle the fires of love:

- Remember: Fragrant roses, moonlit walks, and candlelight dinners are all wonderful ways to avoid addressing the real problems in your marriage.

- Communication is key to any relationship. Put down those binoculars, march right over there, and introduce yourself.

- Try buying your husband that watch he's always wanted, and then throwing it in the ocean to show that your love is more important than material things.

- Important: Homemade love coupons are not only fun, but they'll also save you hundreds of dollars when fucking your wife.

- Fresh fruit, fine wine and seafood are all known to arouse the passions. Cover the bed with them one night.

- Spice up your morning routine by shouting "Good morning, wife!" right into your sleeping spouse's face.

- Please, for the love of God, just stop doing that weird chewing thing with your mouth.

- Vary your lovemaking techniques by having make-up sex, break-up sex, and chased-around-the-front-yard-with-a-meat-cleaver sex.

- If you and your partner are having problems communicating, try and switch things up. Have your boyfriend call you an "impotent sack of balding failure," while you call him a "shrill, delusional hag of a woman."

- Why not make a little game out of who has the higher income, with the loser having to clean the bathroom for a year?

- Take your wife back to the place you had your first date, that magical spot in the Colorado Desert where you sipped wine beneath the stars, ran across the sand, and laughed with the ease of children, holding each other tight and—oh wait, that wasn't you. That was Clark and Emily Gundersen of Erie, NY.

Area Couple Not Sure If Sex Was Tantric

SCARSDALE, NY—Following two hours of stilted, uncomfortable intercourse in which the couple started and stopped at various times, Jeff and Kara DiMarco speculated Saturday as to whether they had just engaged in tantric sex. "I'm pretty sure it was tantric," said Jeff DiMarco, adding that he and his wife skimmed an *Esquire* article about tantra last month, and that what they did Saturday was "like that, sort of." "We were definitely breathing together, and I know I didn't climax, even though I came close a few times. And I think we transmitted energy. Honey, we transmitted energy, right?" Wife Kara later told reporters that she was pretty sure her chakra had been stimulated at some point Saturday, but she couldn't say for sure.

Where Are We Going For Our Anniversary?

Same place we think
we got engaged at

Italian-themed restaurant

Dinner then a show, specifically,
Two And A Half Men

The local Anniversarium

Emergency room,
as per usual

Lab where mad scientist
created us

20%

22%

18%

15%

14%

11%

Honey, I'm Not Going To Stand Here And Debate The Merits Of The First Two B-52's LPs In Front Of The Whole Supermarket

Honey. Please. Just drop it. I'm serious, I'm not doing this with you now. We're in the bread aisle of the Food Lion, for God's sake. I'm not going to get sucked in to another one of these stupid arguments again. Not *now*, okay? Not *here*. No, I'm telling you, I don't want to hear anything about the gimmickry of retro '60s hairdos or guy-girl fractured-pop ensembles, certainly not from someone who worships the Cramps, understand? So just stop.

by William T. Mayhew

People are staring. Could you please lower your voice? Honey, if you think I'm going to stand here in the middle of this supermarket and debate you on the validity of the first two B-52's LPs, then you are *sorely mistaken*.

"Why not?" I'll tell you why not: Because everybody with even half a sense of the post-punk/new-wave aesthetic can tell you that there is NO debating this subject, that's why. Hello? "Rock Lobster"? "Planet Claire has pink air"? Any of this ringing a bell, Mrs. Self-Declared Expert-On-All-Things-From-The-Late-'70s/Early-'80s-Athens, GA Underground-Scene? I suppose they were playing CBGB's in 1978 because they WEREN'T cool? Unbelievable. Where's the goddamn coupon for the applesauce? Well, you had it last...

What? Do not bring Ricky Wilson into this. His alternate guitar tunings were more than just a way to cover for the group's lack of a bassist; they were absolutely inte-

> "Do not bring Ricky Wilson into this. His alternate guitar tunings were more than just a way to cover for the group's lack of a bassist; they were absolutely integral to the driving, rhythmic sound of the band, and you *know* it."

gral to the driving, rhythmic sound of the band, and you *know* it. Derivative of Robert Fripp, my ass. The guy played session dates for Tom Verlaine, for crying out loud. Look, I know what you're doing, and it's not going to work. So drop it. What's the next thing on the list? Cheerios. Just help me find the Cheerios so we can—

What do you mean, "Fuck the Cheerios?"

Honey, listen to me, the sooner we get out of here, the sooner you'll stop embarrassing yourself in front of a store full of strangers with your inappropriate behavior and ill-informed opinions on novelty-rock revivalism. Okay? So go find the Cheerios.

"LOVE Shack"? Why would you even bring UP "Love Shack"? That was an MTV hit in, like, 1989. That is completely outside the range of this discussion, honey. Unless we're talking about a recording where the name Chris Blackwell or Rhett Davies is listed after the word "producer," then it's totally irrelevant. And that includes 1982's David Byrne–produced *Mesopotamia* EP. Why can't you get that through your head? Maybe if you weren't so goddamn stubborn all the time—

"Okay then. No, no, go ahead. I'll just stand here next to the English muffins and listen to you do all the B-52's talking, then. You always do anyway, so go ahead. I'm listening."

Oh, *I'm* the stubborn one? Great. I'm the stubborn one. Ha, that's a laugh. Uh, excuse me, hypocrite-check in aisle four? Who was the one who kept insisting last Thanksgiving that that stupid "You're not the only flame" song—which was a duet with DARYL HALL for chrissakes—was a legit Elvis Costello single? Huh? Who was that again? You ruined Thanksgiving for everyone.

For the last time, we are dropping this NOW. That security guard is looking at us. No, sir, we're fine. No need to call the manager. My wife here is just a little stressed out. And doesn't know anything about call-and-response-based American underground bands. Thank you. Carry on.

Okay, honey, we need milk...

WHAT? What did you just say? You're actually claiming Fred Schneider can't carry a tune? Oh, now you've just lost it. I hope they sell antipsychotics in this store, because you have gone right out of your mind. Could DARBY CRASH carry a tune? Could Mark E. fucking SMITH? So the man's a shouter. What does that have to do with legitimacy as a rock and roll vocalist? Yes, the B-52's are a rock band, dear—yes, it's "dance" music, but I would hardly—

I KNOW they combined surf-rock retro with early pop kitsch! I KNOW that! Why would you even feel the need to tell me that? That was the whole idea, you—

Can I finish my sentence? Are you gonna let me FINISH my fucking SENTENCE? Are you gonna—oh. Okay then. No, no, go ahead. I'll just stand here next to the English muffins and listen to you do all the B-52's talking, then. You always do anyway, so go ahead. I'm listening.

Great. Your old standby about how I like Warren Zevon. We're back to his self-titled second LP again, are we? Yes, dear, I realize the Eagles did the backing vocals on "The French Inhaler." That doesn't mean it's not a classic record! JESUS! NO, you are not roping me into DEFENDING the Eagles, okay? You've pulled that one too many times, sweetie—TOO many TIMES!

Look, final word, and then I'm pushing this cart over to the produce section, with or without you. The first two B-52's LPs—yes, BOTH of them—are CLASSIC FUCKING RECORDS and EVERYBODY who has ANY taste in music AT ALL knows that and this is NOT something I am going to fucking DEBATE with you or anyone else in this store. END of discussion. END OF DISCUSSION, Helen! Helen? HELEN—

FINE! YOU do the goddamn shopping, then! I'm going to the car. And YES, I will be CRANKING "Quiche Lorraine" on the stereo when you get there and I'd better not hear ONE WORD from you about it or I swear to God you are never borrowing any of my remastered Robert Wyatt reissues EVER again! GODDAMMIT! EVERY FUCKING TIME WITH YOU, woman! Congratulations, Helen! YOU WIN! Are you happy now? YOU WIN AGAIN! ✒

To Whom Would We Rather Be Married?

15% Ex-wife

22% A different beekeeper

5% That nice man who does the TV weather

13% U.S.S. Enterprise

26% Better job

19% Girl in white dress stepping off ferry 40 years ago

Butterfly Fuck-Swing Filled With Junk Mail

ELMHURST, IL—An adjustable butterfly fuck-swing once used by Nathan Moscone and Sofia Klein-Moscone to have wild and uninhibited sex in myriad aerial positions has been slowly filling up with junk mail over the past several months, the couple reported Monday.

At one time, the young couple considered the butterfly fuck-swing to be their most precious possession. In recent years, however, it has been eclipsed in esteem by Nathan's leather briefcase and Sofia's emerald earrings.

The dozens of credit card offers, coupon flyers, and unsolicited catalogs were first stacked in the butterfly fuck-swing in order to clear off the dining table for visiting relatives, but more mail gradually began to accumulate on the soft vinyl seat designed to cushion the rapid, percussive strokes of lovemaking.

"The wife and I sure had some crazy times on that thing before we had the baby," said Nathan Moscone, 37, motioning towards the adult toy, upon which he had just hung his suit jacket. "But it seems like forever since I turned her upside down in that thing and dripped hot wax onto her vulva. Maybe we can give it another go after we finish the deck. That's taking up all my spare time at the moment."

The butterfly fuck-swing features nylon straps, padded stirrups, a swiveling hook, a crossbar Klein-Moscone used to grasp in the throes of ecstasy, and, more recently, several unread issues of *O, The Oprah Magazine*.

Moved from the couple's bondage room, now a nursery, to the den late last year, the fuck-swing ended up in an ideal location to deposit mail deemed too unimportant for the already full rolltop desk in the corner. Other items, such as a box of edible lubricants and an 18-inch steel-studded leather paddle, were relocated to the attic to keep them out of the reach of the Moscones' active and inquisitive 11-month-old daughter, Abby.

Klein-Moscone, 33, said that she had considered simply throwing out the junk mail, but balked after the last time, when she accidently discarded an important medical bill that had been placed in the butterfly fuck-swing.

> **"'I was just thinking yesterday, Boy, I can't remember the last time I had my fist up my wife's asshole. It happens to every marriage, I guess.'"**

"I swear I'll get to sorting out that mail soon," said Klein-Moscone, who less than two years ago would strap herself into the butterfly fuck-swing at her husband's slightest suggestion, but now only interacts with the sex apparatus when rummaging through it for a Home Depot receipt.

In addition to raising a baby, Moscone said that working long hours, volunteering at their church, and doing yard work leaves him and his wife very little time to read their mail and enjoy exhilarating sadomasochistic fucking through unconventional methods.

"I was just thinking yesterday, Boy, I can't remember the last time I had my fist up my wife's asshole," Moscone said. "It happens to every marriage, I guess."

Also noticeably absent from the couple's sexual repertoire is the bright purple silicone butt plug that, for the past several weeks, has been the favorite chew toy of their Pomeranian, Champ.

"I'd love to give those ankle and wrist restraints another go, but for the life of me I can't remember where they are," said Moscone about a set of chained leather cuffs that are currently being used to padlock a composting bin in the couple's backyard. "And I haven't seen hide nor hair of our cock rings since we were up in Lake Geneva.

We'll have to get some new ones, I guess."

"Well, as soon as the family budget allows for it," he added.

Despite being forced to retire the nipple clamps after the baby started nursing, the pair said they would still consider having exciting and adventurous sex if Klein-Moscone ever returned home from her advanced Pilates class with any remaining energy.

"Last Thursday, Nathan and I wanted to take his penis prison out of the shed to have a little bit of fun before *Dateline*," said Klein-Moscone, referring to a rubber locking male-chastity device. "But, my God, was that shed a mess—we ended up just sorting junk. At least I found our favorite ball gag, which I'm going to hang in the garage so I know how far to pull the minivan in."

Both Moscones hope to get their once-hot sex life back into gear in the spring, pledging to make good use of a leather hood and spreader bar when they try for another baby. 🖉

Marketing Guru Also A Getting-Divorced Guru

NEW YORK—Marketing guru Bob Lippman, 43, is also a getting-divorced guru, colleagues noted Tuesday. "Bob has an incredible knack for identifying branding strategies to connect with a demographic," coworker Ann Lamp said. "He's almost as good at establishing a product's core consumer message as he is at ending loveless, doomed marriages." In the past 10 years, Lamp has won four Mobius Awards and been married three times.

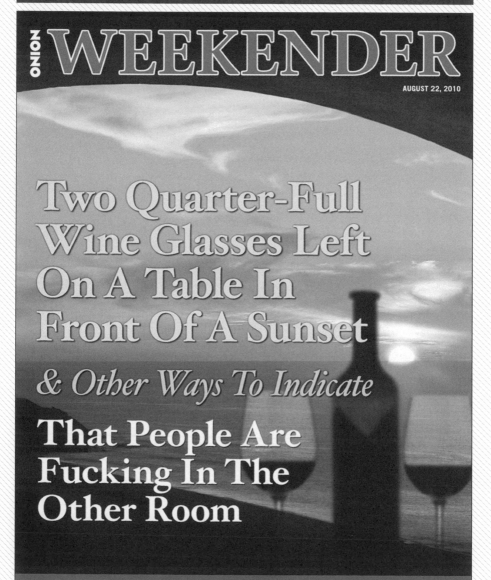

MAGAZINE

ᴼᴺᴵᴼᴺ WEEKENDER

AUGUST 22, 2010

Two Quarter-Full Wine Glasses Left On A Table In Front Of A Sunset

& Other Ways To Indicate

That People Are Fucking In The Other Room

INSIDE Five Charities That Will Give You A T-Shirt When You Donate

Maybe This Appearance On *Jenny Jones* Is Just What My Marriage Needs

My husband Cal and I have been going through some pretty tough times in our marriage lately. For the past three months, Cal's been cheating on me with Rhonda, this 18-year-old stripper who used to baby-sit for us. And just yesterday, after beating me with a tire iron, he told me Rhonda's pregnant and wants us to raise the child.

As you can probably guess, I'm furious at Cal. But I'm not perfect, either. I did, after all, have sex with his father. All sorts of confused

by Ann-Marie Krebs

thoughts run through my head, and I just don't know what to do. My mother thinks I should dump "that piece-of-shit asshole fuck," as she's fond of calling Cal. My best friend Adrienne thinks we should get counseling. I'm thinking an appearance on *The Jenny Jones Show* is just the thing to save our marriage.

I watch Jenny every day, and I really think she could give us the advice and guidance we sorely need. Her show tackles relationship problems like mine all the time, and Jenny's incredible at dealing with them.

First of all, she's full of the plain, common-sense wisdom that all the great daytime talk-show hosts, from Sally Jessy Raphaël to Mother Love, share. I remember one episode where this middle-aged woman was cheating on her husband with her teenage stepson. She said the boy wasn't technically related to her, so what was the problem? I must admit, the woman's argument seemed pretty sound to me.

But Jenny really put things in perspective. First, she asked this lady, "What if your husband was cheating on *you*? Wouldn't you be hurt?" Then Jenny added, "You're this boy's stepmom! Stepmoms aren't supposed to do things like that!" I remember sitting at home in awe. I never thought of it quite that way!

> "Maybe if I come on the show wearing my favorite green dress, someone will refer to me as 'yo, the lady in green.' And maybe someone will point out that I gots to check myself before I wreck myself. Because I do. Sometimes, it takes a stranger in a TV audience to hammer home a point like that."

As great as Jenny is, the studio audience deserves a lot of credit for counseling people, too. They provide just the kind of support system people need when discussing their embarrassing problems on national TV. I particularly remember one audience member's input. The show, titled "I Can't Control My Sexy Teen!", featured a panel of overweight teenage girls who dress like sluts. About halfway through, a male audience member stood up and said to these girls, "Can all y'all ladies say 'choo-choo,' 'cause alls I sees a ho train! Ho!... Ho!... Ho!" Talk about helpful! These remarks let the girls see that their mode of dress was causing them to be treated with less respect than they deserved.

I only pray that such insightful and compassionate people are in the audience if and when Cal and I appear. Maybe if I come on the show wearing my favorite green dress, someone will refer to me as "yo, the lady in green." (The audience always calls the guests it most cares about by the color they're wearing.) And maybe someone will point out that I gots to check myself before I wreck myself. Because I do. Sometimes, it takes a stranger in a TV audience to hammer home a point like that.

If Cal and I do get on *Jenny Jones*, I'm really hoping Jenny springs a surprise guest on us. Like maybe some other woman he's been sleeping with that I don't even know about. That would be great! Then the three of us could sit down and work out our differences by screaming at each other in front of millions of people. That's just the kind of open, loud communication you need in a successful marriage.

I was heartened by the interest I got from *The Jenny Jones Show* when I contacted them recently. Linda, the assistant producer, said my story would fit very well into the upcoming show, "My Man Won't Stop Cheating & Beating!" Linda then asked me if I'd discussed appearing on *Jenny Jones* with Cal. I said no, because he was busy working time-and-a-half at the grain elevator. "That's great," she replied. "Just tell Cal that the two of you are going on *Jenny Jones* because you won the '*Jenny Jones* World's Greatest Hubby Video Essay Contest.' He'll be sure to agree to go on. Then, when Cal comes onstage, everybody will boo him, and we'll reveal the real reason he's on the show—because he's a cheating, beating, lowdown, rotten skunk."

For a moment, I was confused. "Won't that just make him angry at me?" I asked.

But then Linda reminded me of all the hurt Cal had caused me, and said that if anyone deserved a taste of his own medicine, it was him. Well, I couldn't disagree with that logic. Besides, if the audience taunted and mocked Cal the way they did the "Over-80 Transvestites" who were on last week, maybe Cal would see the error of his ways and stop fooling around!

> **"Linda reminded me of all the hurt Cal had caused me, and said that if anyone deserved a taste of his own medicine, it was him. Well, I couldn't disagree with that logic. Besides, if the audience taunted and mocked Cal the way they did the 'Over-80 Transvestites' who were on last week, maybe Cal would see the error of his ways and stop fooling around!"**

So, hopefully, you'll be seeing Cal and me on *Jenny Jones* real soon. There's a chance we may get turned down, which would be terribly disappointing. But if that happens, there are other ways to get the marriage counseling we need. Like by going on *Jerry Springer*. Like Jenny, Jerry always seems to lend a caring, sympathetic ear, and his "Final Thought" is always filled with the sort of solid, time-tested advice that never fails to rub off on guests. ✑

Wife Always Dragging Husband Into Her Marital Problems

HOUSTON —Banker Robert "Rob Boy" Grelman expressed annoyance with his wife, Janet, Monday, saying she consistently involves him in her marital problems. "Every day, it's, 'Oh God, I'm married to someone who doesn't understand me,' or, 'Bob, do you think you could pick up after yourself?'" Grelman said. "Don't get me wrong—I have marriage problems of my own—but I don't know what she wants me to do about hers." Grelman added that his children, following their mother's example, have lately attempted to drag him into their family problems.

Divorced Man Forced To Get Back Down To Dating Weight

SILVER SPRING, MD—Greg Geisinger, a 265-pound Wilmington man whose seven-year marriage ended in divorce earlier this month, must get back down to his dating weight of 190 pounds, he announced Monday. "Oh, man, I have got to lose this weight if I'm gonna be back out there dating again," said Geisinger, who for years has carried 75 pounds of excess marital flab on his 5'11" frame. "No good-looking single woman is gonna want to go out with a guy who looks like this." Geisinger said he is eager to remarry so he can gain back the weight he is about to lose.

Hatred Of Marriage Counselor Brings Couple Together

TEMPE, AZ—Area couple Tom and Becky Witthauser credited the successful resolution of their ongoing marital conflicts to their mutual hatred of their marriage counselor Monday, describing him as the "jag-off whose prissy, ineffectual demeanor brought us closer than we've been in years."

The Witthausers, married eight years, began visiting Dr. Roger Verbicki, 42, a psychologist and accredited couples counselor, in May after months of strife threatened to end their union. Holding hands and gazing lovingly at each other, they described their first fateful meeting with "the insufferable" Verbicki.

"At the time, we could barely make eye contact," Tom said, "But about halfway through the first session, we started casting these sideways glances, because we just hated this guy. We could both feel it."

"After our first session, I told Becky, 'That guy is so unlikeable, like the way he asked us to call him Dr. Roger,'" Tom said.

"And I said I hated him too!" Becky said, finishing Tom's sentence. "He was such a putz, like he's Dr. Phil or something. Our buddy. Gonna help us through this. What a loser."

The Witthausers said they can barely maintain their composure during their weekly meetings, due to Verbicki's various mannerisms and affectations. His nasal voice, sallow complexion, stained teeth, elbow-patched corduroy blazers, and affinity for herbal tea are among the traits cited by the Witthausers. Singled out for particular ridicule was Verbicki's tendency to rest his face against his thumb and index finger and scratch his lower lip.

The Witthausers enjoy a newfound closeness, thanks to their hatred of therapist Roger Verbicki.

Therapist Roger Verbicki.

"I just want to beat the guy up," Tom said.

"And I've really learned to appreciate Tom for that," Becky said.

Tom demonstrated his imitation of Dr. Verbicki, which Becky described as "adorably mean."

"Well, if done in the proper manner, I think it would be very beneficial," said Tom, lampooning Verbicki's frequent use of the phrase "if done in the proper manner" and mispronunciation of the word "beneficial."

The couple laughed and embraced each other.

The Witthausers reported that they started communicating with each other soon after their therapy sessions began, if only to express their revulsion toward their counselor. By spending time together to complain about Verbicki's habits, the couple's romance was rekindled.

"We spent hours walking beside the lake, or drinking wine and listening to music, holding hands, and complaining about the way Dr. Roger's mouth hangs

> **"'We spent hours walking beside the lake, or drinking wine and listening to music, holding hands, and complaining about the way Dr. Roger's mouth hangs open, or how he taps his knees every time he gets up out of the chair.'"**

open, or how he taps his knees every time he gets up out of his chair," Becky said, adding that the mutual sentiments helped the couple realize how much they still enjoyed each other's company and how indispensable they were to each other.

"I can't imagine trashing Dr. Roger with any other person, really," Tom said. ✐

Same Jumbotron Used For Marriage Proposal Used To Ask For Divorce

CLEVELAND—Seven years after using the giant television screen to propose marriage, Kevin Kalish, 36, used the Sony Jumbotron at Jacobs Field to ask his wife Diane for a divorce Sunday. "DIANE, YOU'RE A WONDERFUL WOMAN AND YOU'VE BEEN VERY GOOD TO ME," read the message, posted before 22,347 fans during the fifth inning of an Indians–Royals game. "BUT LATELY I'M JUST FEELING TRAPPED AND SMOTHERED BY MARRIED LIFE. DIANE, WILL YOU BE MY EX-WIFE?" The Jumbotron went on to inform Diane that Kevin assumes she will want custody of their two children, and that he has no plans to contest that.

My Beloved, Would You Do Me The Honor Of Becoming The Fourth Mrs. Charles Ballard?

My dearest Rachel, we've been through so much in the past eight months. We've loved together, laughed together, and grown ever closer. You are everything I look for in a new wife: beautiful, intelligent, strong-willed, and creative. I can't imagine a life without you. So now, down on bended knee, my beloved, I ask you: Will you make me the happiest man alive by doing me the honor of becoming the fourth Mrs. Charles Ballard?

by Charles Ballard

I only told you about Veronica and Patrice? Well, I'm sorry. Janice and I got an annulment after a week, so I usually don't count her. Please, I was so young. It's ancient history. But when I look into your eyes, Rachel, I see our future. I see us living a perfect life in the house that I got from Veronica in the settlement. Unless Veronica gets a better lawyer, I have no doubt that you and I will spend many fine years there.

I know you want to raise a family, and I can't wait for you to meet Travis, Jason, Andrew, Mike, and Charles Jr. The boys are going to love you. And, my darling, as you know, one of the things I value most about our relationship is that we can be honest with each other. That's why I feel comfortable telling you now that I had a vasectomy when I was 35. Patrice insisted on it.

Yeah, she was nuts.

I can honestly say that these eight months have shown me what true love can be. It doesn't have to be predictable and boring like Patrice, or contentious and competitive like Veronica. And there is no reason

for love to be like try-to-run-you-down-with-a-riding-lawn-mower-because-you-forgot-to-return-a-video Janice, but I'd rather not talk about that. Our love is on a completely different level. You are the woman I want to spend the rest of my life with, the fourth and final Mrs. Charles Ballard. I mean, I'm really hoping it turns out that way.

> "[Love] doesn't have to be predictable and boring like Patrice, or contentious and competitive like Veronica. And there is no reason for love to be like try-to-run-you-down-with-a-riding-lawn-mower-because-you-forgot-to-return-a-video Janice, but I'd rather not talk about that."

I want to take you away, my love. Have you ever dreamt of a glorious, two-week honeymoon in the Greek Isles? I've heard it's very beautiful, very romantic, better than Paris. Paris was way too crowded—it's not as great for honeymooning as everyone says. Oh, and obviously, Vegas is out. Yeesh, Vegas. That was a bust. Seriously, I think the Greek Isles is the way to go. Or we could go somewhere else I've never honeymooned before, like Cancun. Why don't you just think about it?

If you accept my humble offer, I will make you so happy. I'll do everything in my power to make sure you never regret that you married me. It's much too painful when that happens.

By the way, I know you wanted a big church wedding, but I really can't get married in a Catholic church again, after Veronica. It's not so bad, though. You wouldn't believe how nice a civil ceremony can be if you put some effort into it. And not to keep harping on this, but I really wish you would reconsider a small wedding with close family and a few friends. Take it from me, the big weddings really aren't worth the hassle and expense.

I just love you so much. Our relationship is so strong—stronger than the other marriages. You complete me in ways my other wives never did. We're always growing together—which is essential, believe me. By now I kinda have it all down. Yup, I think I've seen just about every mistake a wife can make. And I'm better for it! Don't you see? The path of marriage and divorce, marriage and divorce, marriage and divorce has led me to you, at last. And ending up with you has made the journey worth it.

So, Rachel Montesanto, will you make me the happiest man on earth and become Mrs. Charles Ballard *numero quattro*? Ø

Elderly Couple Dresses Up For Trip To Denny's

VERO BEACH, FL—Wishing to look nice for their evening out, Vero Beach retirees Abe and Bernice Wanamaker dressed up Monday for dinner at a local Denny's. "I think I'm going to put on my light-blue slacks before we go," said Abe, taking off the shorts he'd been wearing all afternoon while sitting in the backyard. "And the brown Hush Puppies." Bernice chose to wear her good yellow dress, which she had not worn since a March 22 trip to Lums.

Couple Forgets 70th Wedding Anniversary